Praise for
Financial Darwinism

"The world's political and economic uncertainties, exacerbated by a serious lack of financial transparency, can lead business leaders to feel like they may be virtually flying blind in a rapidly changing global economy. Leo Tilman offers some important tools to address the clear imperative of better strategic and systemic risk management."

William E. Brock
Former United States Senator
United States Trade Representative
and United States Secretary of Labor

"History is littered with the wrecks of financial institutions. Some failed to change their strategies. Others pursued tantalizing returns while paying insufficient attention to the risks. Judging from recent financial crises, many financial institutions still have not learned how to avoid crippling, perhaps even life-threatening, wrecks. Leo Tilman's timely book is a navigator's manual for managers of 21st-century financial institutions. To prosper, even to survive, Tilman clearly and forcefully shows that they must abandon outmoded strategies, adopt new ones, and pay much more attention to the trade-off between risk and return. He blends theory with experience to show how this can be done, and even how it has been done."

Dr. Richard Sylla
Henry Kaufman Professor of The History
of Financial Institutions and Markets
Professor of Economics
Leonard N. Stern School of Business,
New York University

Financial Darwinism

*Create Value or Self-Destruct
in a World of Risk*

LEO M. TILMAN

WILEY
John Wiley & Sons, Inc.

Published by John Wiley & Sons, Inc., Hoboken, New Jersey.
Published simultaneously in Canada.

For general information on our other products and services or for technical support, please contact our Customer Care Department within the United States at (800) 762-2974, outside the United States at (317) 572-3993 or fax (317) 572-4002.

Wiley also publishes its books in a variety of electronic formats. Some content that appears in print may not be available in electronic books. For more information about Wiley products, visit our web site at www.wiley.com.

Library of Congress Cataloging-in-Publication Data:

Tilman, Leo M., 1971-
    Financial Darwinism : create value or self-destruct in a world of risk / Leo M. Tilman.
        p. cm
    Includes bibliographical references and index.
    ISBN 978-0-470-38546-3 (cloth)
    1. Financial services industry.   2. Risk.   3. Value.   I. Title.
    HG101.T55 2009
    332.1068'1–dc22

                                            2008028065

Printed in the United States of America.

10 9 8 7 6 5 4 3 2 1

For Alisa and Owen

Contents

Foreword

The great economic theorist at Chicago, Frank Knight, observing American business experience, took the unprecedented position in his 1921 classic *Risk, Uncertainty and Profit* that most business decisions, especially strategic ones, are to varying degree steps into the unknown. Each of the possible outcomes of a business venture can be considered to have some probability of occurring, but those probabilities are not known to the players. Thus was born the concept of *Knightian uncertainty*. The great theorist at Cambridge and Knight's contemporary, John Maynard Keynes, produced major ideas on the consequences of such uncertainty in his 1921 book *Essay on Probability* and in his 1936 book *The General Theory*.

Knightian uncertainty does not stem from some failure to study on the part of decision makers. Rather, it results from the unknowability of some of the conditions, present and future, on which the consequences of the decisions depend. If gamblers keep betting heads or tails, the evolving holdings may be knowable in a probabilistic sort of way. In the world of Knight and Keynes, though, the economic future is, in large part, not even probabilistic—it is to an important degree indeterminate. And if the probabilities governing the future cannot be known to a participant, they cannot be known to an outside observer or theorist, either. The driver in Keynes's "general theory" is entrepreneurs' intuition about the profitability of investments they contemplate; with their limited understanding, his entrepreneurs can have little idea what the correct expectation of profitability would be.

The heightened uncertainty and indeterminacy in economic life that Knight and Keynes captured came with the rise of the modern economy in the last decades of the nineteenth century. The arrival of finance capitalism, with its restless experimentalism, created *economies of dynamism*—economies with a propensity to innovate in ways that prove viable. It is this new dynamism that radically increased the unknowability that the actors in these economies had to confront. Dynamism—and the accompanying uncertainty and indeterminacy—were virtually unheard of in the so-called *traditional economies* of the eighteenth century. In those economies, uncertainties seldom intruded except in the case of exogenous forces—the occasional scientific discovery, a natural disaster, and so forth. In contrast, in the modern economies that followed, new commercial ideas—thus elements of unknowability and uncertainty—were generated by the operation of economies themselves. From time to time some businessperson, observing current practice first hand, would hit upon an original idea for a better way to do things. First in Britain, then on a wider scale and with greater force in Germany, and later the United States, finance capitalism generated a torrent of endogenous innovations from the 1860s onward for decades—a torrent that in the United States stretched through the 1930s and has had significant recurrences since.

The importance of economic dynamism, though not measured directly, is manifest in several ways. It injects new kinds of activity into business life: employment in the financing, development, and marketing of new commercial products for launch into the marketplace and a cadre of managers deciding what to produce and how to produce it. It appears to lift job satisfaction and employee engagement. It increases turnover in the ranks of the economy's largest firms, as some new firms grow large and displace old firms. Last but not least, it lifts productivity onto a higher (whether or not a faster growing) path. It must be emphasized that rapid growth for a time is not evidence of much or any dynamism; and slow growth for a time is not evidence of a lack of it: Dynamism and growth are not synonymous.

The importance of dynamism in understanding and appreciating the standout economies—going back more than a century—are no secret among economists and business historians. It has been present for years in the pages of Friedrich Hayek, Alfred Chandler, Richard Nelson and Sidney Winter, Roman Frydman and Andrzej Rapaczynsky, Amar Bhide, Virginia Postrel, and some work of mine. Yet the general public has been led to believe the myth that high productivity, wages, and wealth are driven by the great technological advances of unworldly scientists operating outside the nation's economy: Columbus, Magellan, Watt, Volta, Faraday, Marconi, von Neumann, Berners-Lee, and the rest. It has to be mentioned that large numbers of economists find it inconvenient to recognize originality and novelty in their formal economic models. Empirically, however, we do not find that productivity growth arrives in great waves, each linked to a scientific breakthrough. Furthermore, looking across countries, we do not see the patterns that the popular myth would predict: There are wide gaps in productivity levels and in some of the other manifestations of dynamism. It is clear that, in many countries though not all, something big is going on besides science—namely, ideas for new commercial products and new ways to produce.

Historically, capitalism—despite its many imperfections and episodic malfunctions—has proved the premiere economic system for dynamism. Capitalism is all about commercial innovation—the birth of the idea, the development and marketing, and the adoption. Once key freedoms, supporting institutions and favorable attitudes have evolved, some participants step forward with entrepreneurial proposals, others step into roles as lenders or investors to finance some of these projects, still others, as managers or consumers, evaluate and sometimes make pioneering adoptions of the new products.

Of course, the uncertainty and the learning costs entailed by economic dynamism make business life treacherous, though exciting and challenging. There are hazards in acting without allowance for one's limited understanding. Unfortunately, it has become the style in business decision making to pretend that the economy and the financial markets are well understood and that the pertinent numerical parameters of financial and economic models, including the relevant probabilities, are fully known (or close enough to it). The misadventures of recent times—the monetary policy blunders, regulatory mistakes, astonishing financial losses, and worldwide systemic financial crises—are dramatic evidence to the contrary.

The recent problems in the banking sector in the United States are indicative of some of the failures. While many believed for some time that subprime lending and securitization would enable more people to own homes, decision makers had no foundation on which to estimate either the valuations or the risks of the novel assets acquired. Mistakenly, many thought that portfolio diversification could eliminate Knightian uncertainty as well as other risks. Furthermore, models did not allow for macroeconomic swings and for the unknown numbers of new financial companies that might enter the business. The irony here was that the financial sector, in the practices it introduced to capture what it thought were opportunities for a pure profit, ended up creating new and colossal uncertainties for itself and the global economy.

Capitalism has thus been disgraced precisely in the area of its greatest competence. The relatively capitalist economies, notwithstanding the considerable dynamism that classic capitalism showed in its glorious past—the knack for efficient and profitable innovation—have betrayed a lack of awareness and sophistication about what is required for making successful decisions of an innovative nature. Yet we can hope to find in the faults of standard practice and governance some ways to reorient the financial sector toward business development and commercial innovation—with resulting dividends in increased dynamism in the economy. As I have argued for some time, an economically advanced country is not doing justice to the potentialities of the population for self-actualization and self-discovery if it does not examine institutions, attitudes, and beliefs for ways to shore up its dynamism.

This original and provocative book by Leo Tilman therefore comes in our hour of need. It starts off by making sense of the tectonic shift that occurred in finance over the past quarter century. It then proceeds to offer a decision-making framework for operating in the new financial world. Tilman argues that the mechanism of how economic value is created and destroyed in finance is central to understanding modern financial institutions and capital markets. Equally intriguing, he proposes that it is the dynamism of financial institutions' risk-taking and business decisions that both distinguishes the modern financial world from prior financial regimes and serves as the main determinant of their success going forward. He calls this evolutionary thesis *Dynamic Finance*.

This thesis contrasts the brave new world of finance with the old regime of the post-WWII economy. In the past, Tilman argues, financial institutions used to fulfill their chartered roles in ways that, from the risk-management perspective, were very traditional and static. Measures of economic success based on accounting earnings and standard financial disclosures may have been the adequate lens through which to view reality in the good-old days of the banker George Bailey in Frank Capra's *It's a Wonderful Life*, to borrow the author's apt image. However, they are not applicable to the new dynamic state of affairs and thus often lead to confusion and inoptimal decisions. This depiction reminded me of the "traditional economy"—the economy of routine captured by the neoclassical models of economic equilibrium: they excluded change for which there was no prior information and departures for which there was no known knowledge to go by.

The modern economy opens the door for individuals to exercise their creativity by venturing to do something innovative—financing, developing, and marketing of new products and methods. Models of such an economy must recognize the nonroutine ways in which market participants make decisions or deploy resources. These models must also be general enough to be compatible with the myriad of ways in which market participants might revise their views of the future and act on them. In applying a similar line of thinking to financial institutions, Tilman develops a concept of risk-based economic performance that underlies the book's evolutionary thesis and leads to a decision-making framework that he calls *Financial Darwinism*. This book introduces a new intellectual paradigm that can be used to guide strategic and investment decisions. Importantly, however, by recognizing the essence of dynamism, it does not impose the author's views or advocate any particular paths to success, leaving it to financial executives to use their creativity, proprietary knowledge, and ingenuity when ultimately deciding what is best for their firms.

This brings me back to the interaction of uncertainty and dynamism. Given that nonroutine business decisions are steps into the unknown, I have always found it odd that financial executives seemed to think so little about Knightian uncertainty. Tilman does not view this fact as surprising at all, attributing it to old mental paradigms and static business models that obscured the roles of risk taking and uncertainty during the old financial regime. He argues that, as a result of the tectonic financial shift, active risk taking has become a much greater contributor to economic value creation, and, therefore, the role of risk in the lives of financial institutions must be made explicit. Tilman points out that the greater complexity of today's financial world stems from more dynamic economies, more dynamic financial institutions, greater connectivity of the capital markets, and a set of other powerful secular forces. Therefore, the nature of executives' strategic vision and their understanding of uncertainty must change accordingly.

Leo Tilman and I first met at the World Economic Forum in Davos and have since continued our discussion of economic dynamism and the attendant uncertainties at Columbia's Center on Capitalism and Society. From the start, Tilman and I were intrigued by the many parallels between economic dynamism and the dynamism in finance. He sees the latter as essential for modern financial institutions' survival and success. I see the former as the key determinant of a nation's success and, in the age of globalization, maybe its survival. Economic dynamism is invaluable both for high productivity and employment—which serve in turn to increase the inclusion of people into the commercial economy—and for meeting some of our most basic needs: to exercise our imaginations, to enjoy the mental stimulus of change, to have an endless series of new problems to solve, to expand our capabilities, to feel the thrill of discovery, and to experience personal growth.

I believe this thought-provoking book—in interpreting major financial trends, in pointing to the need for financial dynamism, and in providing the relevant arsenal of ideas and decision-making tools to that end—will be of great interest to a broad range of executives, investors, regulators, academics, and students of economics and finance. If Tilman's new paradigm is embraced, financial institutions will be more dynamic. The present banking crisis is both a danger and an opportunity. Let us hope that the banking industry will be given the opportunity to reform itself: to acquire the strategic vision and management practice that will create real and lasting economic value, thus benefiting shareowners, employees—indeed, the whole society.

Edmund S. Phelps
McVickar Professor of Political Economy, Columbia University
Director of the Center on Capitalism and Society, Columbia University
Winner of the 2006 Nobel Prize in Economics.

Preface

"It is not necessary to change. Survival is not mandatory." When it comes to the world of modern finance, this timeless quote from W. Edward Deming is more relevant than ever—and broader in scope than it seems. In fact, financial institutions' willingness and ability to change—and, more generally, the *dynamism* of their business and risk-taking decisions—have become the critical determinants not merely of their survival, but also of their success in creating economic value and benefiting all stakeholders.

This book seeks to help financial institutions adapt to the new financial order. It explains the nature of the tectonic financial shift that has taken place over the past quarter century. It distills strategic, investment, regulatory, and public policy implications of the "future that has already happened."[1] It explores why and shows how financial firms must continuously evolve amidst genuine complexity and uncertainty in order to survive and remain competitive. Last, it identifies actionable ways of putting new ideas into practice in a risk-focused manner.

This book is about *blue ocean strategies*[2] of value creation in finance. It is about change, and change is always difficult—indeed wrenching. Institutions must be redesigned, outdated paradigms discarded, and corporate cultures redefined in the process. However, the alternative—the Darwinian failure to evolve—is far more painful. This is when capital markets, clients, and counterparties beat you to the punch and make difficult choices *for* you, setting in motion self-fulfilling prophesies that often lead to financial ruin.

The ideas underlying this book emerged in the course of my strategic advisory work with financial executives and institutional investors around the world over the better part of the past decade. The detectable origins of the manuscript itself date back to late 2005, when it was the perplexing duality of the financial landscape that gave me the final impetus to start putting new thoughts, observations, and common themes on paper. If you recall, that particular time period was characterized by the tranquility of macroeconomic and market environments, global economic expansion, and impressive financial innovation—all seeming testaments to globalization at its best. New financial markets were growing by leaps and bounds. New assets—ranging from air rights to equipment leases to subprime mortgages—were being securitized, expeditiously blessed by credit rating agencies, and sold around the world. Hedge funds and private equity firms were employing an incredible amount of leverage and dominating financial markets. Investors from New York to Taipei, Munich, and Buenos Aires were dabbling in increasingly complex financial instruments. The financial industry was happily obliging on all counts—and raking in record profits in the process. According to some financial pundits and news commentators, there were all reasons to believe that a combination of skillful monetary policies, regulation, financial engineering, and risk management rid the world of financial instability forever. Needless to say, developing a sense of urgency, seeking introspection, and embarking on difficult organizational changes when life is this good is not easy.

Amidst the bliss, however, something profound was happening behind the scenes, making many of my clients and colleagues increasingly anxious. In sharp contrast to record profits, margins on traditional financial businesses were under severe pressure. Fees for basic financial services were compressing across the board. Competitive pressures were intensifying as the world was becoming increasingly "flat"[3] and flooded with information. The origins, implications, and potential permanence of the low-return environment (dubbed *conundrum* by then–Federal Reserve Chairman Alan Greenspan) were not fully understood. The word *normalization* was frequently used to describe the *hope* that the financial regime would revert to something more familiar. Most importantly, the choices facing financial executives were unclear. Were they supposed to retrench and wait for the world to come to its senses? Were they supposed to radically transform their companies; and if so, how?

This book analyzes the dominant global forces behind the tectonic financial shift and then comprehensively explores the challenges facing financial institutions as well as the universe of their potential responses. Conceptually, it consists of two highly intertwined parts. The first one, presented in Chapters 2 and 3, is the evolutionary thesis (*Dynamic Finance*) that deals with the origins and drivers of the profound changes in the global financial landscape. I propose that the basic key to understanding the behavior of modern financial institutions and capital markets lies in the recognition of the fact that the *process of economic value creation in finance has undergone a fundamental transformation*. More specifically, due to significant margin pressures on basic financial businesses, *active risk taking has begun to play an increasingly dominant role in how financial institutions create (and for that matter destroy) shareholder value*. In order to demonstrate this, I introduce the so-called *risk-based economic performance equation* that helps depart from the outdated accounting-earnings-inspired mental paradigm. Throughout, the *dynamism* of risk-taking and business decisions is emphasized as a distinguishing characteristic of the new world vis-à-vis the old financial regime.

Managing modern financial institutions is a task of enormous uncertainty, scope, and complexity. Thus, the second part of this book (Chapters 4 and 5) uses the evolutionary perspective of *Dynamic Finance* to introduce an actionable decision-making framework (*Financial Darwinism*) that is designed to help financial executives respond to the modern-day challenges. Together, the decision-making framework, the evolutionary thesis, and the risk-based economic performance equation filter out the complexity[4] of the financial world and give financial executives a menu of broad choices on how to create or enhance economic value. They help define strategic vision that properly integrates customer-related and risk-taking decisions, thus unifying business strategy, corporate finance, investment analysis, and risk management. Last, they help determine an *optimal* way to implement the strategic vision using the entire arsenal of advanced financial tools. In the process, risk management naturally becomes the very language of strategic decisions.

This book is intended for a broad audience of executives, financial practitioners, institutional investors, analysts, academics, financial journalists, regulators, and policy makers. Because in today's globalized and competitive world all companies increasingly take on financial risks, many of the ideas should also be relevant to senior decision makers and professionals at nonfinancial companies. Last, this book is written for individual investors and students in finance who are interested in understanding broad financial and macroeconomic trends as well as the challenges faced by the diverse participants in the global financial system.

This work has many theoretical and practical undercurrents, institutional examples, and lessons learned. Because of that, we felt that outlining main ideas in broad strokes prior to getting into technical details was important. Thus, *Chapter 1 is a self-contained, non-mathematical, big-picture overview of the entire book.* Technical readers who are eager to dive into a more detailed discussion as soon as possible may skip the last six sections of Chapter 1 and proceed straight to Chapter 2.

■ ■ ■

Writing this book—and applying the underlying ideas to the real-life challenges facing leading financial institutions, institutional investors, and nonfinancial companies worldwide—has been a truly exciting intellectual journey that spanned many years. I have tried to convey the timeliness and importance of the subject matter at hand on the pages that follow. Meanwhile, the global financial crisis that erupted as this book was nearing its completion amplified the sense of urgency and in many ways validated the premise and proposed approaches. I hope that the readers will find this book engaging and relevant, and I look forward to their feedback. Needless to say, any errors (stemming from the previously mentioned urgency, excitement, or otherwise) that undoubtedly remain in this book are entirely mine.

LMT
New York
April 16, 2008
lmt@FinancialDarwinism.com
www.FinancialDarwinism.com

Acknowledgments

I have been immensely fortunate to benefit from the ideas, advice, and generosity of so many colleagues, clients, and friends. Without their insights, encouragement, and occasional visceral disagreements, writing something as broad-based as this book would not have been possible.

I am greatly indebted to Wade Barnett, Jamie Stewart, Simon Adamiyatt, and James Wilk for their friendship, support, intellectual partnership, and numerous contributions to this work.

This book would have undoubtedly been far more incoherent and incomplete without my developmental editor, Herb Addison. It was Herb's pointed inquiries and ideas that led to many examples and explanations in the book. It was also he who greatly improved the flow and helped make the book suitable for a wide readership with diverse backgrounds.

I owe special thanks to Daniel Spina and Bennett Golub for their friendship and collaboration during my tenures at Bear Stearns and BlackRock, respectively. Dan's vision, creativity, and support were integral in creating within Bear Stearns the role of Chief Institutional Strategist that unified corporate finance, investment, balance sheet management, risk management, and other forms of strategic advice across the firm's institutional clients. Ben's uniquely broad expertise in economics and finance greatly influenced my belief about risk management being a cornerstone of investment and corporate finance decisions, and his extensive review and comments on the manuscript benefited this book a great deal.

I would like to express my sincere appreciation to the following colleagues who spent countless hours carefully reviewing the manuscript and offering invaluable feedback and suggestions: Christian Gilles, Francesco Ceccato, Darrell Duffie, Rockwell Stensrud, Emanuel Derman, Shaun Wang, Bob Engel, Ian Jaffe, Alexandra Sheller, Roger Kline, Michael Patterson, David Moss, Martha Goss, Kevin Hennessey, William Long, Nawal Roy, Alex Pollock, Steven Strauss, Scott McCoy, and Marc Barrachin. I am very grateful to the following colleagues and clients whose input and ideas have affected my thinking in many ways: Mark Abbott, Steve Begleiter, Keb Byers, Michael Buttner, Eugene Cohler, Conrad DeQuadros, Paul Dimmick,

Anthony Faillace, James Hagan, Thomas Ho, Christopher Koppenheffer, Steve Kugelmass, Sang Bin Lee, Jerome Lienhard, Steven Luttrell, Thomas Marano, Jeffery Mayer, Mary Miller, Edward Minskoff, Michael Mutti, Peter Niculescu, Craig Overlander, Leslie Rahl, Robert Rose, John Ryding, Craig Sedmak, Richard Shea, Warren Spector, Makoto Takashima, and Doug Williams. I am very thankful to William Long for his editorial and research contributions, to Renu Aldridge and Elisa Marks for their help with media relations, to Leonor Cantos for her administrative help, and to Kyle Finnerty and Michael Ben-Zvi for their research assistance.

Many aspects of this book have been greatly enhanced in the course of my collaboration with the executive leadership and colleagues from the World Economic Forum, particularly Professor Klaus Schwab, Kevin Steinberg, Gian Carlo Bruno, Paul Smyke, David Aikman, and Martina Gmür.

I am very grateful to Pamela van Giessen, Kate Wood, Kevin Holm, and the entire Wiley team for their enthusiasm and support of this project; and to Dr. Mark Goulston, Lally Weymouth, Keith Ferrazzi, Joshua Ramo, Polly LaBarre, and Josh Waitzkin for helping shape the vision for this book and its audience.

Last but most certainly not least, my utmost love and gratitude go to my wife, Alisa, and son, Owen—who make it all worthwhile.

CHAPTER 1

Understanding and Navigating the Financial Revolution

Introduction: The Need for Transformational Thinking

The world of modern finance is beset with complexity, dynamism, and risk. On a path of ever-intensifying evolution, it presents a landscape of significant uncertainty but also of rapid innovation and opportunity. More so than ever before, success rests on the ability to make sense of the evolutionary changes, link up seemingly unrelated phenomena, and understand the global forces at play. There is a lot to absorb indeed. Once-comfortable financial businesses are confronted with the increased competition and lower margins. Time-tested strategies are being threatened by disruptive technologies and globalization. Financial crises that are deemed "once-in-a-lifetime" by financial models seem to be occurring with an alarming regularity. Sensationalist news headlines and prognostications of financial pundits are obscuring, rather than illuminating, the reality. Worse yet, there is no coherent paradigm to help financial executives, investors, practitioners, and regulators around the world wrestle with these universal challenges and navigate the ongoing tectonic financial shift.

During a recent Harvard Business School seminar, a well-known investor observed that "traditional asset-allocation strategies are having trouble in today's world." A Wall Street executive echoed the sentiment during a TV interview: "being a great M & A advisor alone doesn't cut it anymore. Unless you can also provide a client with a [multibillion dollar] financing package, you're irrelevant." "If you want to stay alive in the asset management business," an equity analyst wrote in a research note, "you have to go into unique products and go out on the risk spectrum." "We've had a tremendous golden age of [commercial] banking, and we are not going to continue to see that kind of performance," concluded the head of a government agency in the United States.[1] Similar urgency is often conveyed behind closed doors of

executive offices and boardrooms—in relation to lending activities, the fight
for bank deposits, secular fee compression, declining margins of traditional
financial businesses, tougher global competition, and increasingly discerning and informed consumers. The resistance to acknowledge the dramatic
and permanent structural transformation of the world of finance—along with
the seemingly accelerating pace of change and innovation—is entirely understandable: Change is hard work. Deep down, however, executives and
investors know—some more viscerally than others—that the new financial
order demands decisive actions on the part of those who want to avoid
becoming casualties of financial natural selection.

My purpose in writing this book was to make sense of this new
realm in which financial institutions and investors find themselves and
to describe—in both theoretical and practical terms—how they can adapt
and prosper. The more conceptual portion of this work is *Dynamic
Finance*—an evolutionary thesis about the origins, the drivers, and the implications of the ongoing financial revolution. The practical part of this
work is *Financial Darwinism*—an actionable decision-making framework
that draws on this evolutionary perspective to help financial executives and
investors navigate the dynamic new world. This chapter is a nontechnical
overview of the entire book that is designed to introduce the underlying ideas in broad conceptual strokes. Figure 1.1 presents this book at a
glance.

The Transformation (Chapters 1 and 2)

Today, huge pools of capital freely roam about the global financial system in
search for investment returns. Capital markets and financial institutions play

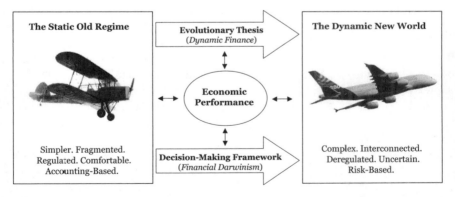

FIGURE 1.1 The Book at a Glance

an increasingly important role in the lives of consumers and real economies. Financial markets are more efficient and interconnected than ever before. Financial instruments and financial institutions are opaque and complex. The static, fragmented, heavily regulated, simpler, comfortable, and accounting-based financial regime has given way to a dynamic, chaotic, globalized, heavily interconnected, deregulated, complex, uncertain, and risk-based realm.

The Evolutionary Thesis (Chapters 2 and 3)

It has been argued that financial services represent an evolutionary system in which no formula works forever: "today's successes will be tomorrow's failures unless they adapt and innovate."[2] In this spirit, *Dynamic Finance* endeavors to comprehensively explain the process of economic value creation by financial institutions. With the ultimate objective of guiding strategic decisions, it examines how financial institutions used to created economic value in the past and then uses financial theory to offer a concise new approach to thinking about economic performance in today's world. In the process, as the multitude of drivers that put pressures on traditional financial businesses is discussed, I argue that many of these forces are secular in nature i.e., expected to last over very long time frames. This makes the return to the comfortable old world of finance highly unlikely.

The Decision-Making Framework (Chapters 4 and 5)

By drawing upon this evolutionary perspective *Financial Darwinism* blends business strategy, corporate finance, investment analysis, and risk management to give financial executives a menu of broad choices on how to create or enhance economic value. Complexity is filtered out, while the richness of unique circumstances and institutional landscapes is preserved. Throughout, I argue that the strategic vision of today's executives must encompass business strategy, dynamic risk taking, and business model transformations—the new concept introduced in the book. This, in turn, requires an expanded skill set on the part of senior decision makers as well as their command of the entire arsenal of advanced financial tools. Importantly, many leading companies are already adapting to the changed financial landscape in the general spirit of this book's ideas, even in the absence of a comprehensive framework. These desirable evolutionary responses pose a stark contrast to the notable failures to recognize the new realities and adapt accordingly, as demonstrated by modern financial crises and other institutional experiences with sad endings.

The Conceptual Anchor

In the center of it all—linking the seemingly disparate macroeconomic and financial market phenomena as well as institutional behaviors—is the concept of *economic performance* and its own evolutionary transformation. The old-fashioned, accounting-earnings-inspired formula for economic performance was reflective of the buy-and-hold nature of traditional financial businesses. I propose that the basic key to understanding the behavior of modern financial institutions and capital markets lies in the recognition of the fact that the process of economic value creation in finance has undergone a fundamental transformation. More specifically, due to significant margin pressures on basic financial businesses, active risk taking has begun to play an increasingly dominant role in how financial institutions create and destroy shareholder value. Therefore, the analytical expression for economic performance should change accordingly. The introduction of the *risk-based economic performance equation* enables the development of both the evolutionary thesis and the resulting practical decision-making framework underlying this book.

The Role of Risk Management

One of the important motifs of this book is the convergence of business strategy, corporate finance, investment activities, and risk management under the umbrella of executive decision making. Risk has always been a major factor in financial transactions and the lives of financial institutions. However, as any practitioner would attest, a palpable disconnect between risk management and executive decision making has largely persisted with risk management often viewed as a policing function or a passive safety-and-soundness verification. More often than not, the risk manager continues to be brought in *after* major strategic decisions had already been made. It is, therefore, not surprising that despite the advances in financial theory, analytics, and technology that afforded an increasingly rigorous understanding of complex portfolios and balance sheets, elevating risk management to be an important decision tool has proven challenging. On the pages that follow, I explain why pressures on traditional financial businesses are likely to become a catalyst for changing the mental paradigm underlying executive decisions, with active risk taking and risk management becoming explicitly linked to the process of economic value creation. It is imperative that risk management becomes the very language of enterprise-wide strategic decisions going forward and that the chief risk officer becomes an executive who gets an equal seat at the table where corporate strategy is decided.

In order to set the stage for the discussion of the old financial regime and the way it worked, let us look next at a classic American film that takes us back to the origins of the world of finance as we know it.

From George Bailey to the Golden Age

My students and colleagues are often puzzled with the frequency of my references to one of the most beloved American cinema classics, *It's a Wonderful Life* (1946). To me, however, in addition to bringing reflection and a sense of purpose to so many viewers every holiday season, this film is indispensable in any discussion on the evolution of the financial system and the nature of financial intermediation. Next time you immerse yourself in the film's nostalgic snow-covered world of Bedford Falls, you just might see certain aspects of this life-affirming story through a different lens.

The life of George Bailey (Jimmy Stewart) is neither prosperous nor carefree. In fact, we first learn about him on a Christmas Eve through the prayers of Bedford Falls' residents. Overwhelmed by his misfortunes and "worth more dead than alive," George is contemplating a suicide. As the movie progresses, we realize that George's life—as that of his father who started and ran the Bailey Brothers Building and Loan Association—is a far cry from "lassoing the moon and bringing it down." More than anything, George wants to leave the "crummy little town," see the world, go to college to "see what they know," and then do something big and important. Instead, he devotes his life to running the "measly, one-horse institution" where people can come to borrow money. George sends his brother to college in his place, marries his childhood sweetheart, spends his honeymoon money on averting a bank run, and fights the "the richest and meanest" man in town, Mr. Potter (Lionel Barrymore), to keep the building and loan association going. What drives him is a deep-seated belief that hard-working people deserve to "work and pay and live and die in a couple of decent rooms and a bath."

An angel (Second Class) is dispatched to save George by showing him how much he has contributed to the lives of so many. As they walk through the town seeing what life would be like if George had never been born, they discover that Bedford Falls (named Pottersville, instead) is a dystopian nightmare. The Bailey Brothers Building and Loan Association is long closed, Bailey Park with pretty homes for the working families has never been built, and Ma Bailey, his mother, is running a boarding house. As George realizes that his life has had a profound effect on the town and returns to his family, the Bedford Falls residents rush to his rescue with their savings—more than making up for the funds his uncle mistakenly lost. In an inspirational and deeply spiritual ending, as the camera glances over the pile of money on the table, we see George—happy and at peace—with his little daughter in his arms (and her flower petals in his pocket). In the way that matters, he truly is "the richest man in town."

The world of finance—along with its evolution toward the Golden Age witnessed toward the end of the twentieth century—has come a long way from the time depicted in "It's a Wonderful Life." George could not have known that home ownership would become a major public policy objective in the United States and an amazing source of wealth creation for the population as a whole. Nor could he have imagined that 60 years later a complex network of securities firms, commercial banks, and government-sponsored enterprises would pool together, securitize, guarantee, make markets, slice and dice, and sell mortgages, credit card receivables, and student loans of Bedford Falls' residents to investors in Rio de Janeiro, Abu Dhabi, Beijing, and Moscow.

Gradually, throughout the latter half of the twentieth century, macroeconomic and financial landscapes evolved toward more sophisticated regulation as well as more deliberate public and economic policies. Toward the end of the century, financial businesses became more institutionalized. Risk-management practices and tools improved. Economic volatilities—swings in unemployment, output, inflation, and interest rates—declined. Regulation greatly enhanced the safety and soundness of financial intermediaries, protecting their clients and stakeholders. The power of the informed and discerning consumers steadily increased, and client service became one of the key ingredients of success (*pace*, Mr. Potter).

Among other benefits and apart from rare exceptions, this allowed executives running financial institutions to spend honeymoon money on honeymoons as opposed to averting bank runs. While the good times were occasionally interrupted by rocky periods—such as the inflationary experience of the 1970s, the Savings and Loan crisis of the 1980s, and the Asian and the Long-Term Capital Management crises of the late 1990s—everything culminated in what can be described as a Golden Age of financial intermediation. Why is that? While the external environment dramatically improved, *fees and other forms of compensation for basic financial services generally remained handsome*, inspiring such old saws about the banking businesses as: "Borrow at 2 percent, lend at 6 percent, and be on the golf course by 3:00 pm." George Bailey would have liked that!

Interestingly, as financial intermediaries were becoming convinced that the Golden Age would never end, a tectonic shift was already underway. The financial landscape changed significantly—slowly at first, and then gaining speed—and a vast array of new financial products and services began competing in an increasingly complex and global marketplace. Margins on traditional businesses began to decline, forcing financial institutions everywhere to start exploring ways to adapt to the unfamiliar new world.

Accounting for Profits the Old-Fashioned Way

Before I turn to the discussion of the tectonic financial shift itself and the evolutionary changes that it brought about, I want to look more closely at the process of shareholder value creation by financial institutions during the old regime. On the surface, of course, success was measured by their ability to generate stable and growing *accounting* earnings. Deep down, not surprisingly, powerful economic considerations were at play. They represent a critical building block of this book's evolutionary perspective.

It all starts with the so-called flows of funds and risks that describe the mechanism according to which assets of consumers and companies become liabilities of others, and vice versa.[3] For instance, a commercial bank may take in customer savings as deposits. These deposits (consumer assets) thus become this bank's liabilities. In turn, the bank may take the funds received through deposits and loan them out as mortgages, at which point these loans become the assets of the bank and liabilities of the corresponding borrowers. Insurance companies may take in premiums from insurance policies (assets of the insured parties and liabilities of insurance companies) and invest them in bonds or stocks issued by non-financial corporations. Pension plans would receive sponsor contributions and invest them in various assets with the intent to satisfy liabilities to their beneficiaries in the future. In the process, most financial institutions would charge their customers various fees. Banks would collect deposit account charges as well as loan and servicing origination fees. Meanwhile, insurance companies would impose policy surrender changes and asset management fees, brokers would collect trading commissions, while investment banks would earn underwriting and advisory fees.

Notice the following dominant feature of the basic financial activities during the Golden Age depicted in Figure 1.2. A financial institution's profitability is largely determined by (a) the difference between how much is earned on the assets net of how much is paid on its liabilities, (b) plus the fees it earns, (c) minus its operating expenses, and (d) minus its cost of capital. Importantly profits over the long haul—and the very viability of financial institutions—depend on the difference in *economic* returns between assets and liabilities. The focus on economic—as opposed to accounting—returns here is critical: The shortcomings of accounting earnings have been widely commented on in the business press and in the financial literature,[4] and the potential for divergence between accounting and economic realities can be especially dangerous, as I describe more fully in Appendix B.

Given the nature of traditional financial businesses the economic performance of financial institutions during the old regime can be thought of as the following simple expression:

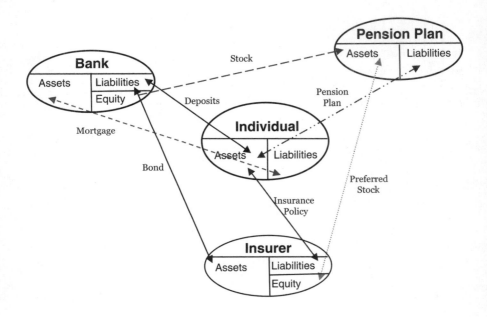

FIGURE 1.2 An Illustrative Old-Regime Closed Financial System

$$\text{Economic performance} = \text{return on assets} - \text{cost of liabilities} + \text{fees}$$
$$-\text{expenses} - \text{cost of capital}$$

Despite its simplicity, this economic performance equation provides interesting insights into the past practices of financial institutions—and the corresponding ways of thinking. First, notice that for institutions that create economic value in this fashion to be viable and profitable, *the combination of fees and differential asset/liability returns needs to be sufficiently high relative to expenses and cost of capital*. This was indeed the case during the Golden Age of financial intermediation. The implication of the banker joke, for instance, is that what an institution earns on assets (6 percent) is so much larger than what it pays on its liabilities (2 percent) that it more than makes up for other expenses, producing a handsome return on capital.

A more general description of the mode of operation that is based on differential returns between assets and liabilities is known in the financial industry as the *carry trade*. Carry trades are infamous and very simple indeed: An investor or a financial institution borrows money *cheaply* (e.g., in the countries where interest rates may be low at the time) and invests it in higher yielding loans or securities, pocketing the profit. The deceiving ease with which earnings can be delivered through carry trades has been deeply ingrained in the minds of investors and professionals across financial sectors. Banks, insurance companies, real estate investment trusts, money managers, investment banks, and even pension plans and non–financial companies often think about certain segments of their businesses as carry trades. The term itself is very visual. While the asset is simply being *carried* on the books—without any hedging or dynamic management—the owner has the privilege of receiving the difference between the asset's yield and the cost of funds. Imagine a check just showing up in the mail every month—a bonus of sorts.

Given the very nature of basic financial activities described above, the *strategic vision* of executives at that time was related to their *business strategy and corporate finance* activities, whereby they sought answers to questions like these: What parts of the business should we invest in for optimum growth? What is our desired business mix? When should we retrench and when should we become aggressive in sizing up our balance sheet or our customer activities? How can we improve customer service and the underwriting process in order to reduce credit losses, maximize asset/liability returns and fees, and control expenses?

As a consequence, the risks taken on by financial institutions remained generally the same over time. That is, *from the risk-management perspective, business models of financial institutions during the Golden Age can be characterized as static.* In this case, the word *static* refers to the traditional ways in which financial institutions deployed their balance sheets to fulfill their chartered roles in the financial system. Static also indicates the absence of dynamic risk-taking behavior and is not to be confused with management's innovative uses of M & A, customer service or retention strategies, new product development, cross-selling, or expense management—all directed at growing static businesses in a cost-efficient manner. The focus on the delivery of stable and increasing accounting earnings through the growth of static (from the risk-management perspective) businesses implied that accounting earnings and business strategy combined with corporate finance represented the two pillars of strategic decision making during the old regime, which is summarized in Figure 1.3.

Why are the previously-mentioned economic performance equation, the banker joke, carry trades, and focus on accounting earnings all the artifacts of the old regime and outdated ways of thinking? It is because lurking behind the differential returns between assets and liabilities—the cornerstone of the prevailing mental paradigm—is a plethora of hidden financial risks! More often than not, it is these underlying financial risks that

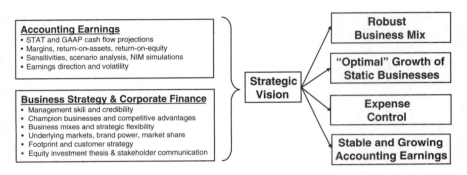

FIGURE 1.3 The Two Pillars of Strategic Decisions in the Static World

lead to the differences in returns between assets and liabilities—a far cry from a riskless check in the mail.

What can be inferred about these hidden risks inherent in static business models during the old regime?

- These risks were direct consequences of a financial institution's role as an intermediary within the financial system.
- They were masked by accounting earnings, not always understood, and not actively managed over time.
- Since many of these risks are inherently cyclical—related to cycles in the economy as a whole—the earnings of financial institutions often experience an attendant cyclicality.

Risk taking has always played a very important role in the lives of financial institutions. However, accounting standards, buy-and-hold practices, and the old mental paradigms often obscured the true nature of risks inside of static business models. That may have been adequate when competitive pressures were lower while fees and the compensation for taking financial risks were high, as was indeed the case during the Golden Age. However, when fees and arbitrage opportunities decline and the compensation for risk taking compresses, the room for error declines accordingly, revealing the cyclicality and volatility of static business models and at times forcing financial institutions and investors into vicious circles of greater leverage and risk taking.

Last, static business models also help explain the historical disconnect between executive decision making and risk management. Consistent with the nature of strategic objectives during the old regime (Fig. 1.3), risk management was not a strategic tool but rather a process brought in *after* business decisions had been made to check on their potential risks. Thus, as risk measurement and management tools became progressively more sophisticated, so did the after-the-fact safety-and-soundness exercises. Yet the decision-making paradigm remained largely unchanged.

The "Great Moderation" As an Evolutionary Catalyst

The following quote from the recent work by Niall Ferguson and Oliver Wyman helps set the stage for this book's evolutionary perspective on finance:

> *Financial history is, in sum, the result of institutional mutation and natural selection.... Financial organisms are in competition with one another for finite resources (customers, clients, market share). At certain times and in certain places, certain financial species may become dominant. But innovations by competitor species, or the emergence of altogether new species, prevent any permanent hierarchy ... from emerging.... Institutions with a "selfish gene" ... will tend to endure and proliferate....*
>
> *Nevertheless, this process is not wholly endogenous. Periodic exogenous shocks can radically alter the evolutionary environment, rendering certain evolved traits disadvantageous that previously had been advantageous, and vice versa. Financial disruptions (like the Great Depression of the 1930s or the Great Inflation of the 1970s) are like the asteroid strikes and ice ages that periodically intervened in the evolutionary story of life on earth. In extreme cases, they can cause mass extinctions of financial species; in milder cases, when environmental change is more gradual ... they eliminate the less fit members.[5]*

In order to rigorously explore the challenges facing modern financial institutions, this book proposes the following *evolutionary thesis* referred to as *Dynamic Finance*. During the benign macroeconomic and inflationary environment dubbed the "Great Moderation"[6] (approximately 1985–present), a set of powerful forces that I will describe in a moment changed the financial landscape significantly, diminishing the viability of static business models and putting pressures on traditional financial businesses. In the process, active risk taking became an increasingly influential contributor to how financial institutions create and destroy shareholder value.

Importantly, unlike such prior evolutionary catalysts as the Great Depression of the 1930s and the Great Inflation of the 1970s, the Great Moderation has been a long and gradual environmental change accompanied by a marked decrease in economic volatility—at least, that appeared to be the case until the 2007–2008 financial crisis. Wild swings in unemployment, economic output, inflation, and interest rates have been seemingly tamed by globalization, financial innovation, risk management, and skillful monetary policies. The tranquility of the macroeconomic environment, the gradual nature of the tectonic financial shift, and the record profits of the Golden Age all obscured the profound nature of the change and provided little urgency to even acknowledge it, not to mention adapt to it.

Similar to the aftermath of previous financial "asteroid strikes and ice ages," those financial institutions that will survive and prosper this time around will do so by adapting to the new environment in a way that parallels the natural selection of Darwin's biological organisms. In this regard, the *dynamism* of risk-taking and business decisions in finance is a distinguishing characteristic of the new world compared to the old financial regime and a major determinant of success in the future.

As the first step in describing the pressures on basic financial services and identifying desirable evolutionary responses on the part of financial institutions, it is important to understand the conglomeration of powerful global forces that came to the forefront during the Great Moderation. I classify these forces into three distinct groups—secular, period-specific, and cyclical—and briefly outline them below. They are discussed in further detail in Chapter 2.

First, I examine the group of 10 secular forces that affected financial institutions during the Great Moderation. As before, in this context, *secular* refers to the long time frame over which these factors are expected to influence the global financial system.

1. *Globalization of capital markets and financial services* has turned a collection of "heavily controlled, segmented, and sleepy domestic financial systems" into "lightly regulated, open, and vibrant global financial system."[7]

2. *Inflation targeting* and control by central banks around the world contributed to the decline in both levels and variability of inflation and, in turn, was an important driver of the low return environment across financial markets.

3. *Disintermediation*—the process of "cutting out the middleman" whereby corporations, investors, and consumers deal with each other directly and gain more direct access to capital markets—has removed some financial institutions from the traditional flows of funds.

4. *Greater availability of information* has led to most up-to-date market and financial product data becoming broadly disseminated, especially over the Internet.

5. *Greater financial market efficiency* has arguably become increasingly pronounced in normal market environments, stemming from the greater

availability of information, advances in technology, and huge amounts of often-unconstrained capital flowing freely around the world in search for returns.

6. *Alternative investment* vehicles—such as *hedge funds* and *private equity funds*—have dramatically affected the behavior of capital markets, business models of other financial institutions, and the overall leverage in the financial system.
7. *Financial deregulation* (i.e., liberalization) has contributed to the reduction of price controls, portfolio requirements, product restrictions, and barriers to entry within a financial system.
8. *The convergence* (i.e., blurring of the lines) between different traditional financial businesses—a direct consequence of deregulation, disintermediation, and earnings pressures—became pervasive.
9. *Increasingly complex financial instruments* such as *derivatives and structured products* have become an important (and permanent) feature of modern capital markets.
10. *Advances in technology, financial theory, analytics, and risk management* have enabled disintermediation, capital market innovation, "atomization" of risks, the growth of structured products, and the rise of alternative investments.

I refer to the *second group* of forces that greatly affected financial institutions during the Great Moderation as *period-specific*. While at this stage of the new dynamic order the permanence of these factors is unclear, their impact on the financial landscape has been significant and, thus, needs to be articulated:

1. *Disinflation exporting*—the abundance of low-cost labor in developing countries combined with the liberalization of trade—has limited inflation in developed countries and impacted the market environment.
2. The *global savings glut*—a confluence of forces behind a significant increase in the global supply of savings—has facilitated the transition of many developing countries from net borrowers to net lenders and changed the global flow of funds.[8]
3. *Bretton Woods II*—an allusion to the international monetary system with fixed exchange rates between 1945 and 1971—has represented the adoption by several countries, mostly in Asia and the Middle East, of currency exchange rates that were pegged to the U.S. dollar. This, in turn, has affected financial institutions and capital markets worldwide in multiple ways.

While the Great Moderation spanned multiple economic cycles, the third group of the cyclical factors (e.g., economic expansions, favorable corporate and consumer credit fundamentals, flat yield curves, low volatilities) has at times exacerbated the pressures on traditional financial businesses brought about by secular and period-specific forces. This is especially relevant to understanding the dynamics of modern financial crises, as discussed later in the book.

Economic Performance in the Dynamic New World

So what was the net impact of these forces on the global financial system and, by extension, on real economies, financial institutions, and capital markets? In the spirit of "Don't try this at home" (i.e., not meant to be studied too closely), Figure 1.4 illustrates the challenges at hand.

Globalization of capital markets, disintermediation, alternative asset managers, securitization, and other secular forces have fundamentally changed the traditional flows of funds and risks. The dynamics of the global financial markets—and the latent feedback loops—became infinitely more complex. Financial products and financial institutions themselves became more sophisticated and opaque, with disclosures about their inherent risks increasingly outdated. Margin pressures on traditional financial businesses with static business models increased, leading to institutional responses

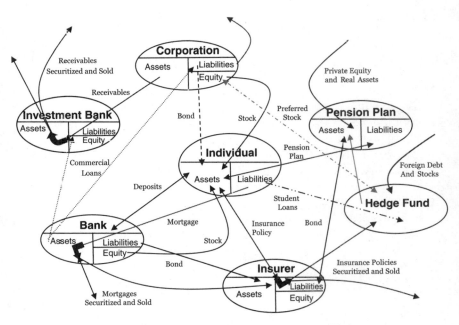

FIGURE 1.4 The Chaotic, Intertwined, Opaque, Dynamic New World

where increased leverage and risk taking were not always understood. Thus, in order to describe this new world of finance and adapt to it, a radical break with past thinking and acting—of the kind that Thomas S. Kuhn called a *paradigm shift* in his influential book *The Structure of Scientific Revolutions*—is needed. More specifically, an actionable framework must be developed where: (a) the complexity is filtered out, (b) evolutionary insights into the process of economic value creation are explored, and (c) strategic alternatives available to financial executives are examined.

The discussion on potential evolutionary responses by financial institutions to the new environment brings us back to the concept of economic performance—and its own much-needed transformation. Recall criticism of static business models and the corresponding old ways of thinking about economic value creation. First, during the Golden Age, business strategy and corporate finance were the primary decision tools used to grow traditional businesses and maximize accounting earnings. Second, risks underlying business models were not always understood and were not actively managed over time, which often resulted in cyclical earnings. Third, the disconnect between executive decision making and risk management persisted despite advances in analytics and technology. To illuminate these shortcomings and describe how financial institutions can adapt, the old-fashioned concept of economic performance needs to be updated to reflect the modern-day realities. In particular, the changed role of active risk taking in delivering economic performance and the nature of risks inherent in various business models both need to be made explicit.

A simple analytical transformation of the old economic performance equation discussed in detail in Chapter 3 affords useful insights into the process of economic value creation in the dynamic new world. It focuses on the differential returns between assets and liabilities, showing that underlying this accounting-inspired construct are three distinct components —balance sheet arbitrage, principal investments, and systematic risks:

Return on assets − cost of liabilities

   = balance sheet arbitrage + principal investments + systematic risks

This observation leads to the new *risk-based economic performance equation* that reflects the changed role of risk taking in the process of economic value creation:

Economic performance

   = balance sheet arbitrage + principal investments + systematic risks

   + fees − expenses − cost of capital

Economic performance in the dynamic new world is generated through balance sheet arbitrage, principal investment activities, exposures to systematic risks, fee-based businesses, cost-control, and minimization of the cost of capital. This description represents the process of economic value creation in terms of conceptually different risk-taking and fee-generating activities, which I refer to as *risk-based business models*. Here, briefly, are the components of the risk-based economic performance equation.

Balance Sheet Arbitrage. The ability of some financial institutions to borrow funds at submarket levels is obviously a rare and very desirable feature in the era of efficient capital markets. While this book's use of the word *arbitrage* may offend finance purists, it simply alludes to institutional features (e.g., the charter or the nature of business) that help generate profits on the liability side of the balance sheet without putting significant capital at risk, which is a significant competitive advantage. Common examples of balance sheet arbitrage include lower-than-wholesale rates paid on retail deposits of commercial banks as well as funding advantages enjoyed by some government-sponsored enterprises. The introduction of this new component of economic performance allows us to conceptually separate customer-related corporate finance activities from active risk taking. Additionally, balance sheet arbitrage helps explain why not all carry trades are created equal. In many cases, differential returns between assets and liabilities are due to inherent financial risks rather than balance sheet arbitrage.

Principal Investments. As a response to the pressures facing static business models, financial institutions are increasingly risking their own capital in order to enhance economic value created by traditional financial businesses. Per the risk-based economic performance equation, such risk taking falls into two distinct categories—*principal investments* and *systematic risks*. The difference between the two lies in the *types of risks* that are undertaken in the attempt to generate economic performance, which has important implications for the corresponding organizational structures and risk-management tools. Thus, principal investments include direct private equity and venture capital stakes, investments in hedge funds and private equity funds, or capital allocations to internal proprietary trading desks. According to my adopted convention, principal investments are assumed to have no *structural* systematic risk exposures over time. Macro-level decisions involving principal investments (their broad categories, sizes, and risk limits) are often made by senior executives at financial institutions. However, specific investment decisions are often decentralized, with traders, portfolio managers, or private equity fund managers implementing their own views on the markets and securities subject to risk limits and other guidelines. This is why, consistent with financial theory, diversification is used as a primary risk-management tool when it comes to portfolios of principal investments of real-world institutions and investors. Not surprisingly, greater allocations of capital to principal investment activities require significant organizational changes and typically entail larger risks, greater complexity, and the lack of transparency for external stakeholders.

Systematic Risks. In addition to principal investments, the dynamic management of *systematic risks* is playing an increasingly important role in the lives of modern financial institutions. The dynamism of this process (also known as *market timing* in the investment analysis arena) is a critical feature here since it directly addresses the shortcomings of static business models characterized by unmanaged (structural) risk exposures. Systematic risks are related to whole economies or markets and cannot be eliminated via diversification. Correlations among different systematic risks vary over time and tend to increase in times of crisis. Common examples of systematic risks include interest rates, credit risks, mortgage prepayments, currencies, commodities, and equity indices. According to some financial theories, an institution's expected return for bearing a systematic risk over a given holding period can be represented as the product of (a) how much risk it has taken on, and (b) how much it gets paid for taking on a unit of risk. The systematic risk component of economic performance explicitly links dynamic risk taking and value creation and is central to the explanation of the pressures facing traditional financial activities. In short, clinging to static business models in periods of declining compensation for risk taking may create vicious circles of greater leverage, especially if other parts of the economic performance equation come under pressure at the same time. I contend that systematic risk taking is very different from other activities of financial institutions. First, it relies on investment analysis and modern risk management to a much greater extent. Second, it must be managed in a centralized fashion at the top executive level; for example, taking on more interest-rate risk and less equity or credit risk on the balance sheet may be deemed desirable if the economy is expected to go into a recession. Third, this type of active risk taking requires significantly different executive skill sets, decision-making processes, and analytical systems. It is very different from, say, the task of assembling a diversified portfolio of investments in hedge funds that endeavor to profit from buying "undervalued" securities and selling "overvalued" securities.

Fees and Expenses. These components of the economic performance equation are self-explanatory: Financial institutions remain focused on growing fee-based businesses and controlling expenses. Of special relevance for business model and economic performance discussions, the importance of fee-based businesses tends to increase—with the fight for them intensifying—whenever the differential returns between assets and liabilities decline.

Capital Structure Optimization. This component of economic performance—alternatively described as *the minimization of the total cost of capital*—has become increasingly visible in recent decades as financial institutions have been afforded tremendous flexibility with respect to debt funding and capital raising alternatives.

Pressures on Static Business Models

Having introduced the risk-based economic performance equation, we can now proceed to a more detailed discussion of the challenges facing static business models. Thus, as the secular forces began to gather momentum during the Great Moderation, pressures on traditional financial businesses began to intensify. At times, as illustrated by the U.S. institutional experiences listed below, these secular evolutionary changes in the financial environment were exacerbated by period-specific and cyclical factors.

- Net interest margins (differential returns between assets and liabilities) of U.S. commercial banks have declined by 25 percent over the past 15 years. This fairly persistent compression was due in part to the increases in both the relative costs of liabilities as well as their sensitivity to changes in interest rates. In risk-based terms, this can in part be described as the compression of the *balance sheet arbitrage* component of economic performance.
- Dangers of static business models were illustrated by the experience of the U.S. life insurance industry in 2000 to 2003. During that period, investment returns declined and competitive pressures increased. In response, most insurers invested in progressively riskier instruments and issued liabilities with increasing amounts of embedded short options. During the subsequent recession, these greater risks did significant damage to the industry's capital and earnings. In 2001 to 2002, realized losses of 20 top life insurers in the United States amounted to almost

$11 billion, with average return on assets dropping to below 2 percent in 2002. This episode—that can be described in terms of pressures on the *systematic risks* and *fees* components of the economic performance equation—showed the susceptibility of static business models to secular compression in fees coupled with low-return environments.

- The experience of defined-benefit pension plans in the United States during the first decade of the twenty-first century was equally troublesome—and also related to unmanaged *systematic risks* inherent in static business models. Historically, pension asset allocations were heavily skewed toward equities, which was contrary to the fixed-income nature of their liabilities. Given these exposures, a simultaneous drop of equity prices and interest rates hurts pension plans the most. Between 1999 and 2007, assets of pensions with traditional static asset allocations grew by 33 percent, while their liabilities grew by over 110 percent over the same time period.[9] Thus, a pension plan that was fully funded in 1999 would have been underfunded by 37 percent in 2007—entirely because of the static asset allocations and underlying mismatched risks between assets and liabilities. The latter calculation is consistent with the actual experience of U.S. defined-benefit pensions.

- Throughout the Great Moderation, other traditional financial activities have experienced a dramatic *fee* compression. Representative investment bank underwriting fees declined by 70 to 80 percent between 1997 and 2007. Equity trading commissions charged by brokers decreased by 80 to 90 percent over recent decades. According to anecdotal evidence, loan origination fees, bid-ask spreads, clearing fees, and asset management fees for large institutional mandates experienced a similar fate, albeit to a lesser extent.

- The low-return environment in 2003 to 2006 coupled with a secular *fee* compression resulted in a wide range of financial institutions attempting to earn additional returns via complex financial instruments with significant underlying *systematic* market and credit risks. During the subsequent financial crisis, prices of these securities dropped precipitously amidst deteriorating economic fundamentals, the lack of market liquidity, and incapacitated structured-product markets. Between September 2007 and April 2008 alone, write downs across commercial banks, securities firms, and insurers amounted to over $200 billion. As a result, capital ratios declined and the total capital in excess of $65 billion had to be raised during a market dislocation, leading to higher overall *costs of capital* and impairing future economic performance.

Representative pressures on static business models during the Great Moderation are summarized in Table 1.1.

TABLE 1.1   Pressures on Static Business Models During the Great Moderation

Financial Sector	Pressures on Static Business Models	Magnitude/ Time Frame	Relevant EP Components
Commercial Banks	Margin compression	−25% (1992–2007)	Balance sheet arbitrage Systematic risks
Life Insurers	Margin compression	−22% (1997–2007)	Systematic risks
Brokers	Decline in trading commissions	−88% (1980–2007)	Fees
Investment Banks	Decline in underwriting fees	−76% (1997–2007)	Fees
Life Insurers	Realized losses due to excessive risk taking in response to secular pressures and a low-return environment	−$11B (2002–2003)	Systematic risks Fees
DB Pensions	Decline in funding status due to mismatched A/L risks	−50% (1999–2007)	Systematic risks
Securities Firms Commercial Banks Insurers	Significant write downs due to excessive risk taking in response to secular pressures and a low-return environment	−$200B+ (2007–2008)	Systematic risks Fees

Note: Corresponding references and data sources are presented in Chapter 2.

The risk-based economic performance equation affords us with insights into the exact sources of pressures on traditional financial businesses that came to the forefront during the Great Moderation. It helps explain why risk and return characteristics of static business models have increasingly become at the mercy of capital markets and economic cycles, with attempts to replenish declining earnings at times leading to vicious circles of leverage and risk taking. Last, it sheds light on the two distinct types of undesirable institutional responses to pressures. The first involved financial executives who hoped that things would return to "normal," questioning the need to adapt and clinging to static business models in the face of evolutionary changes. The second involved financial institutions that attempted to adopt a more active approach to risk taking without appropriate decision-making frameworks, investment processes, and risk-management capabilities in place. As described in the next section, both have proven perilous.

Dynamic Finance Perspective on Financial Crises

Global financial crises serve as an invaluable, albeit extreme, learning experiences about the inner workings of the new world of finance, providing convincing evidence of the profound evolutionary changes that have occurred over recent decades. To elaborate on one of the most telling examples of pressures on static business models from the previous section, let us examine how the stage for the 2007-2008 credit and liquidity crisis was set. We start by systematically describing the impact of global forces on each component of risk-based economic performance.

The Vicious Circle of Leverage and Risk Taking

It is all too tempting to declare the 2007–2008 financial crisis merely a cyclical phenomenon. Consider the following familiar pattern. The late stages of a prolonged economic expansion are accompanied by a period of tranquility and low default rates, leading to the overall complacency on the part of both financial institutions and investors. Underwriting standards on loans and covenants on debt instruments get progressively looser, while access to cheap credit becomes abundant. Risk taking becomes reckless, and imbalances build up. A well-deserved reckoning ensues in due time.

I argue, however, that the unique features of the 2007–2008 crisis suggest that powerful new phenomena—those that extended far beyond the cyclical forces—were at play, causing an unprecedented increase in leverage throughout most of the global financial system. As a way of understanding this, let us walk through the components of the economic performance, one by one.

First, such secular forces as globalization, disintermediation, greater availability of financial information, intensified competition, and increased consumer sophistication decreased the opportunities for *balance sheet arbitrage*. Second, the same factors compressed *fees* associated with basic financial services. To defend against these, financial executives dispatched a variety of corporate finance activities directed at preserving balance sheet arbitrage, reducing *expenses*, and minimizing *the cost of capital*. Meanwhile the growth of *fee-based businesses* (that included asset management and "originate, securitize, and sell" business models) became an important part of supplementing existing sources of earnings.

For many financial institutions, these actions proved insufficient in mitigating the margin pressures. Part and parcel of the buildup in leverage, financial institutions and investors—unwilling to accept lower returns and earnings—turned to greater risk taking. The latter involved both *principal investments* and *systematic risks*. In addition to leveraging static business models explicitly, market participants began to employ alternative investments, progressively more sophisticated trading programs, and complex and opaque financial instruments and derivatives. Due to laws of supply and demand, greater demand for risky investments resulted in the decline in compensation for bearing financial risks.

Meanwhile, the rise in alternative investments—coupled with an increase in market efficiency—led to highly leveraged hedge funds and proprietary desks chasing the same set of investments and further compressing the returns from risk taking. In fact, secular, period-specific, and cyclical factors have *simultaneously affected most components of the economic performance equation!* The following vicious circle ensued: Margin pressures pushed financial institutions and investors to take on progressively larger risks. That, in turn, further compressed the returns from risk taking. Last, in one of the important risk-management lessons learned, what we see in retrospect as greater risk taking was not perceived as such by the market participants during the leverage buildup. Perversely, as market volatility declined, so did the estimates of risk, such as Value-at-Risk, that many institutions used. The reliance of some risk measures on recent historical data signaled to many market participants that an increase in nominal exposures was appropriate. In Figure 1.5 we see this vicious circle in graphic form.

FIGURE 1.5 The Vicious Circle of Leverage and Risk-Taking

In the prelude to the credit and liquidity crisis that followed, the spring of leverage and opaque risk taking was wound up to an unprecedented extent.

The Vicious Circle of Deleveraging

What was the outcome of the failures to adjust static business models to the changing realities or forays into active risk taking without requisite skills, processes, decision-making frameworks, and risk-management capabilities? It was the financial crisis that sent ripple effects across real economies and financial markets around the world. While not all market crises have an easily identifiable cause, the 2007–2008 dislocation was sparked by the housing market deterioration in the United States, coupled with the increase in delinquencies on mortgage loans. Once the crisis got going, however, many of its features had a lot in common with other significant dislocations of the past decade—for instance, the 1998 LTCM crisis—and could be described as follows.[10] First, risk aversion, deleveraging, and the flight to less risky investments all lead to illiquidity in complex positions and accompanying price declines. Business models relying on securitization of loan originations become unviable. Margin calls and forced liquidations directed at meeting these obligations follow. This, in turn, leads to the so-called *contagion* where forced sales of positions occur even in markets that are not directly threatened. Commercial and investment banks become more risk averse and reduce lending activities, creating difficulties for financing in capital markets and forcing additional liquidations. The downward spiral continues as prices decline and margin calls increase, leading to further risk aversion and deleveraging. Similarities in risk exposures, risk tolerances, and risk-management practices across the global financial system become the determining factors, often overwhelming macroeconomic backdrops and prompting the description of these events as *technical* (related to supply-and-demand). Figure 1.6 shows the vicious circles observed during the unwinding stages of modern financial crises.

Complexity, Globalization, and Unintended Consequences

The following additional lessons from the 2007–2008 financial crisis illustrate the evolutionary changes in the global financial landscape and suggest the need for transformational thinking:

- Complex securities used by financial institutions and investors to counteract margin pressures often lack transparency with respect to their underlying risks.

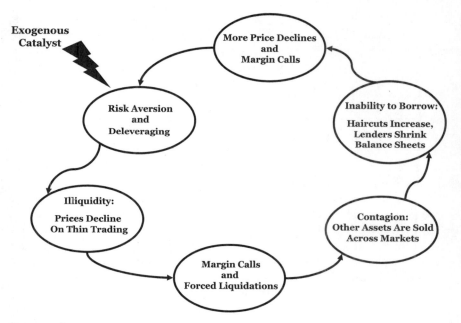

FIGURE 1.6 The Deleveraging Stage of a Modern Financial Crisis

- The increased complexity and lack of transparency also apply to financial institutions themselves due to inadequate financial reporting. They increase stakeholder and lender uncertainty about risk exposures and contingent liabilities of their counterparties, crippling investment and financing environments in times of crisis.
- Non-risk-based constructs—such as credit ratings and accounting earnings—that fail to convey the true nature of financial institutions' business models and risk exposures may be not only unhelpful but actually blinding, contributing to both the winding-up and unwinding stages of financial crises.
- The leverage in the system may be exacerbated if the market compensation for bearing financial risks—already potentially mispriced at the end of an economic expansion—is additionally reduced by period-specific and secular phenomena.
- The quest for higher origination volumes amidst compressing fees and the prevalence of "originate, securitize, and sell" business models that detach originators from credit risk both contribute to the loosening of underwriting standards.

- The global diffusion of risks—coupled with the lack of adequate risk-based financial disclosures—can dramatically amplify the vicious circles of risk taking and deleveraging in a testament to the increased complexity, interconnectivity, and opaqueness of the dynamic new world.

Given the secular nature of many forces at play, continuing pressures on static business models, and the nature of modern mechanisms according to which imbalances build up and then unwind, it is reasonable to expect that systemic financial crises as described may be a permanent feature of the new financial regime.

Pillars of Strategic Decision Making

To understand how financial institutions can adapt to the dynamic new world, recall the prevailing mode of operation that served so well during most of the Golden Age. Static business models produced adequate earnings because of high fees and generous asset/liability spreads. The executives' skill sets were reflective of the dominant priorities at hand: Create a robust mix of businesses through organic development; seek mergers and acquisitions that complement existing businesses; achieve stable and growing accounting earnings; minimize expenses; and grow individual businesses through a variety of customer-related activities. I have referred to this entire process as *business strategy coupled with corporate finance.* Along with accounting earnings, they were previously described as the pillars of strategic decision making during the old regime, as illustrated in Figure 1.3.

Evolutionary changes in the world of finance argue for a fundamentally new approach to economic value creation. The buy-and-hold old-regime mentality must be replaced by a new paradigm represented by the risk-based economic performance equation. *Strategic vision* needs to encompass dynamism, active risk taking, business strategy, and corporate finance all at once. Even after an organization has successfully adapted and transformed itself, it cannot stand still but must continue to reassess and rebalance its resources, businesses, and risks as the market environments change around it.

As active risk taking and dynamic management take on a more prominent role in delivering economic performance, the nature of strategic vision, the concept of optimality, and the nature of companies' communication with stakeholders must all change accordingly. Part and parcel of the expanded mandate of an executive, rigorous risk management becomes the very

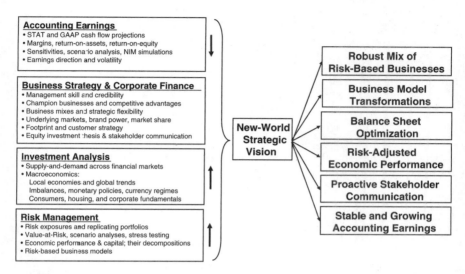

FIGURE 1.7 The Four Pillars of Strategic Decisions in the Dynamic New World

language of strategic decision making and the key ingredient of future success. Greater complexity and uncertainty of the landscape—including strategic alternatives, competitive pressures, and the market environment—necessitate a dramatic change in the required executive skill set. A greater importance is placed on executives' understanding of macroeconomic forces, a rigorous investment philosophy, and a command of advanced financial tools. Therefore, the two pillars of strategic decision making—that during the old regime included accounting earnings and business strategy combined with corporate finance—must be expanded to include risk management and investment analysis, forming the four pillars shown in Figure 1.7. I argue later in this book that movement toward fair valuation and risk-focused regulation are likely to gradually shift the "power equation" away from the accounting-based mentality and toward economic value creation and the risk-based paradigm.[11] This is schematically represented through the arrows in Figure 1.7.

Value Creation Through Dynamism and Business Model Transformations

I began this chapter with the quotes from financial executives dealing with the challenges of the dynamic new world. They questioned the viability of traditional asset-allocation strategies. They argued that, in addition to offering fee-based advice, investment banks have to finance their clients' projects and co-invest alongside them. They urged that asset managers need to continually expand into new asset classes and offer new products to stay competitive. They cautioned that the Golden Age of commercial banking may be over.

When interpreted from the evolutionary perspective of *Dynamic Finance*, these observations are, in essence, descriptions of the pressures facing static business models in a changed world. Along with lessons learned from modern financial crises, they suggest the need to radically reengineer the business models of financial institutions, making them more dynamic and flexible and enabling active risk taking to become a major contributor to economic value creation.

As modern financial institutions and institutional investors are adapting to the new order, executive strategic decisions directed at dynamic economic value creation can be thought of in terms of the following two general categories.

- *Responsive recalibrations of business models*: Transitions from static to dynamic business models, where *individual components* of the risk-based economic performance equation are continually enhanced[12]; and
- *Full-scale business model transformations*: Dynamic rebalancing of risk-based business model mixes on the enterprise-wide level that will be addressed in a separate section later in this chapter.

Here is a closer look at responsibe recalibrations of business models.

Responsive Recalibrations of Business Models

Enhancement of the individual components of the economic performance equation is the important first step in transitioning from static to dynamic business models and changing the corresponding ways of thinking. A combination of business strategy, corporate finance, investment analysis, and risk-management activities can be employed in this regard as follows.

- *Balance Sheet Arbitrage.* This component of economic performance can be enhanced through a variety of business strategy and corporate finance activities. For example, commercial banks can improve customer service, employ cross-selling and customer retention strategies, or enhance brand power and market share in an effort to increase the share of retail liabilities on their balance sheets. This can potentially reduce the overall cost of retail liabilities as well as their sensitivity to changes in interest rates. Meanwhile, government-sponsored enterprises can maintain and enhance funding advantages by continually improving their risk management sophistication, expanding their debt and capital offerings, and actively growing the universe of investors in these securities worldwide.

- *Principal Investments.* Expansion into principal investments starts with a formulation of a strategic vision regarding the role of different types of risk taking in the overall business model. Investment preferences, expected returns, macroeconomic views, and risk budgets can subsequently help optimize the portfolio of principal investments, including capital allocations to proprietary trading, stakes in hedge funds, as well as private and public equity investments.

- *Systematic Risks.* The dynamic management of systematic risks is increasingly used to create economic value across financial sectors. In this regard, financial institutions and institutional investors can employ such organizational structures as asset/liability committees and investment strategy committees to implement this enterprise-wide ("top-down") risk-taking process on a senior management level. Macroeconomic views, investment analyses, risk-management considerations, and advanced financial instruments can all be used to arrive at and subsequently execute such decisions as decreasing interest-rate risk in an anticipation of an economic expansion or decreasing exposures to consumer and corporate credit in anticipations of a recession. In a notable trend, financial institutions are continually adding new asset classes—commodities, hard assets, and local currency emerging markets—to their investment arsenal in order to increase investment flexibility and improve risk-adjusted returns. The increasing importance of the dynamic management of systematic risks in delivering economic performance represents a departure from static business models, significantly affecting the nature of executive decision making and stakeholder communication in the process.

- *Fees and Expenses.* A variety of activities that typically fall under the umbrella of business strategy and corporate finance can be proactively used by modern financial institutions to grow fee-based businesses and control expenses. Of particular importance to this component of economic performance is the advent of securitization—the process of pooling together assets and future receivables, repackaging them as financial instruments, and selling them to investors. During securitization, financial institutions may collect various fees and commissions as well as earn the so-called *deal arbitrage*—the difference between the total value of repackaged securities and the cost of the underlying collateral. Dangers associated with inadequately risk-managed "securitize and sell" business models became apparent during some of the recent financial crises where capital markets that trade securitized products became incapacitated. Securitization has become an important new source of fee income, transforming risk-taking businesses (such as loan origination) into fee-based businesses and presenting many conceptual, organizational, and risk-management implications. As for expenses, financial institutions continue to be proactive and innovative in minimizing them through mergers and acquisitions, technological innovation, applications of the management science, and other business strategy and corporate finance activities.

- *Capital Structure.* Minimization of the total cost of the firm's capital structure has become an important component of economic performance in recent years. Typically, investment banks and other strategic advisors are retained by financial institutions and non-financial companies to analyze the alternatives and subsequently underwrite and sell debt and capital instruments to investors worldwide. Today, when a plethora of funding and capital choices exists—ranging from common and preferred stocks to various forms of debt instruments and hybrid capital securities—capital structure optimization has become a nontrivial act of balancing regulatory requirements, credit-rating considerations, tax strategies, and capital market perceptions. It should be noted that capital structure optimization exercises may simultaneously affect other components of the economic performance equation (e.g., differential systematic risk exposures between assets and liabilities). This suggests that capital management should be a part of an integrated enterprise-wide process.

Leading real-world financial institutions are already responding to the major changes around them. Examples of companies that are making transitions from static to dynamic business models by enhancing the individual components of the economic performance equation are presented in Table 1.2.[13]

Applications to Non-Financial Companies

It is worth noting that the risk-based economic performance equation—used primarily in this book to analyze the economic value creation by financial institutions—also has implications for non-financial corporations. In fact, growing fee-based businesses, minimizing expenses, and optimizing the capital structure are examples of responsive recalibrations of business models that are similar across financial institutions and non-financial corporations. One of the recurring motifs of this book is that management of systematic risks has become an important determinant of economic performance of financial institutions. It is also the case with non-financial corporations that routinely take on financial risks in their international operations, debt issuance, cash management, securitization, capital management, pension-related decisions, and M & A. Failures to properly manage financial

TABLE 1.2   Firms Enhancing Individual Components of the Economic Performance

EP Component	Type of Enhancement	Institutional Examples
Balance Sheet Arbitrage	Growth of retail deposits and improvements in customer service standards	Wachovia
	Debt product innovation coupled with a proactive expansion of the investor base	The Farm Credit System
Principal Investments	Using the firm's own capital to take stakes in other financial institutions	Bank of America, HSBC, RBS, Allianz, ING
	Expansion of hedge funds into private equity activities and vice versa	The Tudor Group, The Blackstone Group, KKR
Systematic Risks	Expansion of the investment universe and dynamic rebalancing of systematic risks according to economic and market views	PIMCO (as asset manager)
Fees	Growth of asset management businesses, which may be coupled with principal investments	Goldman Sachs
Expenses	Using mergers and acquisitions to lower the cost of operations	The Bank of New York Mellon
Capital Structure	Innovative uses of hybrid capital securities	US Bancorp
	Accelerated share repurchase programs	State Street Bank Marsh & McLennan

Note: Corresponding references and data sources are presented in Chapter 5.

risks are numerous and well-documented, with recent notable examples including foreign exchange as well as auction-rate securities-related losses of non-financial companies (Chapter 5). For financial institutions and non-financial companies alike, the concept of risk-based economic performance can help establish the relationship between economic value creation, executive choices, and risk management.

Full-Scale Business Model Transformations

Financial Darwinism encompasses a plethora of executive decisions that help financial institutions adapt to the new reality and enhance economic performance in a dynamic fashion To illustrate the decision-making process and a myriad of alternatives surrounding full-scale business model transformations, consider the following types of choices and dilemmas facing executives at modern financial institutions: Do I grow risk-taking businesses or fee-based businesses? Among risk-taking businesses, do I emphasize commercial lending or principal investment activities? Where and how do I short options to increase my returns? Among fee-based businesses, do I prefer brokerage, strategic advisory, or asset management? What is my view on "originate, securitize, and sell" business models?

It stands to reason that any firm will try to maximize the balance sheet arbitrage and minimize both expenses and cost of capital as per the previous section. Subsequently, as shown in Figure 1.8, the following fundamental philosophical decision needs to be made: *What is the desired proportion of economic performance that should be generated through risk-taking*

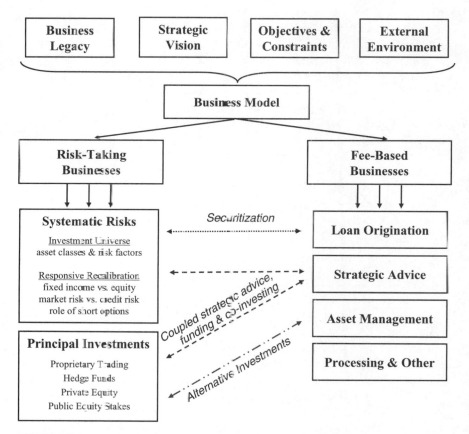

FIGURE 1.8 Example of an Executive-Level Strategic Decision Tree

activities vis-à-vis fee-based activities? This decision should be based on the institution's legacy; unique circumstances, objectives, and constraints; external environment; and, most importantly, strategic vision of executives. It should reflect the overall risk tolerance of the company, its perceived competitive advantages, as well as its risk-management philosophy, dramatically affecting all subsequent decisions.

Let us continue walking through Figure 1.8. After the role of risk-taking activities vis-à-vis fee-based businesses—and their relative desirability—have been determined on a macro level, more specific choices within each category can be analyzed and implemented in the spirit of responsive recalibrations of business models. Within the systematic risk component, after the investment universe is established, risks can be dynamically rebalanced according to macroeconomic and market views. Among principal investment activities, the roles of proprietary trading, stakes of hedge funds and private equity funds, and direct private equity and venture capital stakes can be periodically reassessed. The same process applies to alternatives related to fee-based businesses. Relevant details within different components of economic performance can be further enhanced through more formal optimizations that use analytical computer systems.

Once broad conceptual decisions have been made, the art of marrying business strategy, corporate finance, risk-based business models, and investment decisions begins. At this stage, executives must answer yet another important set of questions. Should strategic advisory services be coupled with principal investment and financing activities, as shown via lines connecting Strategic Advice, Principle Investments, and Systematic Risks in Figure 1.8? Should growth of asset-management (fee-based) businesses be intertwined with principal investments? Should originated loans be retained on the balance sheet as is, or hedged, or securitized and sold, with the latter choices effectively converting a risk-taking business into a fee-based business? What kinds of options should be bought or shorted on the balance sheet?

Today's executives responsible for strategic decisions face a continuous conceptual optimization problem that attempts to help financial institutions arrive at a robust business mix, minimize the cost of capital, preserve strategic flexibility, generate stable and growing earnings, and achieve premium equity market valuation. Making the maximization of absolute and risk-adjusted economic performance an equally important priority can seamlessly integrate *Financial Darwinism* into the lives of financial institutions. The outcome of the decision-making processes described previously is the desired mix of *risk-based business models* that reflects strategic vision of executives as well as numerous objectives, considerations, and constraints unique to the institution. Business strategy combined with corporate finance, risk management, and investment analyses are integrated within a top-down framework that encompasses both business and risk-taking activities. By construction, risk-management executives become active participants in strategic decisions—not a policing function responsible for after-the-fact safety-and-soundless verification.

Not surprisingly, the overall effectiveness of business model transformations depends on the executives' ability to implement their strategic visions through a combination of financial and organizational means. In this day and age capital markets afford tremendous flexibility in enhancing economic performance, solving a particular problem, or arriving at a portfolio of businesses with desired risk/return characteristics. Thus, both the breadth of perspective and the necessary change in the executive skill set repeatedly emphasized in this book become self-evident: In order to determine an "optimal" implementation of an "optimal" strategic vision, an intimate familiarity with the entire arsenal of advanced financial tools is required. As shown in Figure 1.9, leverage strategies, asset management, hedging, securitization, insurance, mergers and acquisitions, capital structure optimization, debt management, and product design are all at the disposal of financial executives today.

Let me close this section with the following comment about the interaction between accounting and economic realities. While this book focuses on economic performance and a risk-based paradigm, the delivery of stable and growing accounting earnings is likely to remain the governing reality and an overriding objective of financial institutions in the foreseeable future. This implies that a practical and realistic approach to implementing the framework that I have proposed involves a simultaneous optimization of both accounting earnings and economic performance. Alternatively,

FIGURE 1.9 The Arsenal of Financial Tools Used in Business Model Transformations

economic performance can be optimized subject to various risk and accounting earnings constraints.

There are reasons to believe, however, that as the world of finance continues moving toward risk-focused regulation, more comprehensive financial disclosures, and fair valuation, the balance of power in both strategic decisions and stakeholder priorities should gradually shift away from accounting earnings and toward economic performance, increasing the importance of investment analyses and risk management as pillars of strategic decision making as shown in Figure 1.7. If this admittedly provocative prediction comes true, this would have the following significant capital market implications:

- As the relevant information about business models, risk exposures, and the entire process of economic value creation becomes gradually available to financial institutions' stakeholders, equity market valuations should become more directly linked to the economic reality rather than accounting earnings.
- Premium equity market valuation should become increasingly reflective of the company's success in translating active risk decisions and business model transformations into economic value creation. Accelerating trends in absolute and risk-adjusted economic performance should lead to expanding valuation multiples over time.
- Perceptions about the future prospects of companies should be increasingly shaped by the risk-based communication between companies and stakeholders. When behaving in the spirit of *Financial Darwinism*, executives will have to proactively and systematically: (a) describe their strategic visions and rationale for business model transformations; (b) articulate the track record of generating consistent and growing economic performance through active risk-taking decisions; and (c) demonstrate that they possess the necessary competency, skills, broad perspective, and command of advanced financial tools.

As with responsive recalibrations, some financial institutions are already undertaking full-scale business model transformations designed to counteract the pressures on static business models. Table 1.3 describes several distinct types of such actions. Think of these examples as adhering to the "spirit" of *Financial Darwinism*—even in the absence of a comprehensive framework presented in this book.

Business model transformations are likely to become a critical component of not only success but the very economic viability of financial institutions and investors in the changed world. They should increasingly contribute to economic value creation, differentiating visionary firms from their competitors and leading to premium valuation in the capital markets.

TABLE 1.3 Organizations Undertaking Comprehensive Business Model Transformation

Financial Sector	Business Model Transformation	Institutional Examples
Central Banks Sovereign Wealth Funds DB Pension Plans College Endowments Insurance Companies	Transition away from static business models via allocations to alternative investments	China Investment Corp. ADIA Yale Endowment Texas Teachers Swiss Re Allstate
Commercial Banks Insurance Companies Pension Plans	Transition away from static business models via dynamic management of systematic risks	Wells Fargo MetLife
Insurance Companies Commercial Banks REITs	Transformation of risk-taking businesses into fee-based businesses via securitization	AIG*
Investment Banks	Coupling of strategic advice with financing and principal investment activities	Goldman Sachs
Commercial Banks Investment Banks	Shorting out-of-the-money options via acquisitions of reinsurance companies or asset-management strategies	Lehman Brothers*
Financial Services	Coupling of brokerage with other fee-based services, such as strategic advice	Marsh, Inc.

Note: SWF stands for Sovereign Wealth Funds Texas Teachers stands for Texas Teachers Retirement System Corresponding references and data sources are presented in Chapter 5.
*Important examples despite the companies' problems during the 2007–2008 financial crisis.

Beyond the Façade: The Importance of Risk-Based Transparency

The lack of risk-based transparency associated with modern financial institutions has become indisputable in recent years. On one end of the spectrum is the increasing number of firms that engage in dynamic risk-taking and business model transformations in order to create economic value. On the opposite end of the spectrum are the financial institutions and investors that continue to cling onto static business models, often responding to pressures with increased leverage and investments in highly complex and opaque financial instruments.

Not surprisingly, traditional financial disclosures—that may have been adequate in informing the financial community and stakeholders about the process of economic value creation during the static old regime—often fail to describe more intricate aspects of behaviors of today's financial institutions. During market dislocations, the lack of risk-based transparency may result in significant stakeholder and lender uncertainty, crippling investment and financing environments. For instance, during the 2007–2008 credit and liquidity crisis, hundreds of billions of contingent liabilities and write downs, proprietary trading losses, concentrated credit exposures, and complex investments by a wide range of institutions and investors have all greatly surprised capital markets and regulators, resulting in an extreme risk aversion across the global financial system and a vicious circle depicted in Figure 1.5.

In Figure 1.10, I illustrate the lack of risk-based transparency in graphic form by contrasting the building façades (metaphors for what outsiders know about financial institutions) with the actual underlying business models. As an adequately disclosed legacy business on the left is transformed into an enterprise reflective of the executives' strategic vision, the business model and its risk/return characteristics can be altered dramatically. However, financial disclosures and the capital market perceptions (building façades) remain largely unchanged, putting the effectiveness of credit ratings, equity valuations, and analyst reports in doubt.

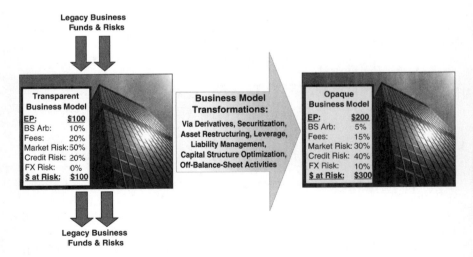

FIGURE 1.10 Beyond the Façade: The Need for Risk Based Transparency

If financial institutions and their stakeholders are to take full advantage of the opportunities of the dynamic new world and mitigate the severity of financial crises, the need for risk-based transparency in the system—direct, clear, and comprehensive descriptions of financial institutions' business models, risk exposures, and economic value generation mechanism—is paramount. A number of initiatives in the realm of public policy, regulation, and accounting standards are currently underway to address this issue.

■ ■ ■

To grasp just how different the dynamic new world is from the post-World War II era that has served financial intermediaries so well, let us now turn in Chapter 2 to the study of the old regime and its inner workings in greater detail. Among other things, this chapter illustrates that W. Edwards Deming was, regrettably, correct: "It is not necessary to change. Survival is not mandatory."

CHAPTER 2

The Old Regime and Its Demise

Economic Performance and Viability of Financial Institutions

In this chapter and those that follow, I revisit in more depth the topics that were discussed in broad strokes on the preceding pages. As will be seen, this inevitably leads to some repetition, for which I make only a weak apology: I suspect that most readers will appreciate being reminded of overarching ideas as they plunge more deeply into various subjects here and in the rest of the book.

So let us return to the discussion on the Golden Age of financial intermediation and look in more detail at how it worked and what happened to it. As before, we start with the flows of funds and risks that describe the mechanism according to which assets of consumers and companies become liabilities of others, and vice versa. In the case of a commercial bank, it may take in customer savings as deposits. These deposits (consumer assets) thus become this bank's liabilities. In turn, the bank may take the funds received through deposits and loan them out as mortgages, at which point these loans become the assets of the bank and liabilities of the corresponding borrowers. Insurance companies may take in premiums from insurance policies (assets of the insured parties and liabilities of insurance companies) and invest them in bonds or stocks issued by non-financial corporations. In the process, most financial institutions charge their customers various fees. For instance, banks collect deposit account and loan origination fees; insurance companies impose policy surrender changes and asset management fees; brokers charge trading commissions; while investment banks earn underwriting and advisory fees.

Notice the dominant feature of these financial activities: A financial institution's profitability is completely determined by (a) the difference between how much is earned on the assets net of how much is paid on the liabilities, (b) plus fees, (c) minus its operating expenses, and (d) minus its total cost of capital (the opportunity cost of funds provided to the firm).[1] Importantly, profits over the long haul—and the very viability of financial institutions—depend on the difference in *economic* (not accounting!) returns between assets and liabilities.

These observations lead us to the concept of *economic performance (EP)*—the anchor of *Dynamic Finance*. Reflecting the very nature of financial intermediation during the old regime, the following definition of economic performance is designed to capture the total economic return generated by all financial and operational activities of a financial institution over a particular time period. *Economic performance is the difference in total economic returns between assets and liabilities, plus fees, minus expenses, minus the cost of capital.*

On the conceptual level:

The Old-Regime Economic Performance Equation

$$EP = R_A - R_L + F - E - C_C$$

where R_A and R_L are total economic (fair-valuation-based) returns on assets and liabilities; F and E are total fees and expenses, respectively; and C_C is the total cost of the firm's capital—all presented in consistent terms (e.g., percentages of current assets). In this regard, the total cost of capital is the weighted average cost of the capital structure, which is reflective of the required rates of returns on the underlying instruments. Notice that while the cost of capital (C_C) is separated from the cost of liabilities (R_L) for now, I will show later in this book that asset/liability management and capital management are inextricably linked and must be a part of an integrated enterprise-wide strategic process.

The readers may find the definition of economic performance just presented reminiscent to the well-known concept of Economic Value Added (EVA), which is typically defined as the difference between Net Operating Profit After Taxes (NOPAT) and the total cost of capital.[2] There is, however, an important difference: In the case of financial institutions, NOPAT and, by extension, EVA are usually based on return estimates that adhere to accounting standards as opposed to economic reality. The components of the economic performance equation presented above are, in essence, economic analogs of the following standard accounting earnings metrics, including those used in EVA.

Economic Performance	Accounting Earnings Analog
$R_A - R_L$	Net Interest Margin – Loan Loss Provision
F	Non-Interest Income
E	Non-Interest Expense
C_C	Required ROA, ROE

As mentioned previously, in order to serve as an appropriate measure of economic value creation, the economic performance equation must be reflective of fair valuation and economic reality. The numerical illustrations of the concept of economic performance and of the fact that economic and accounting realities may diverge significantly are presented in Appendix B.

The concept of economic performance naturally leads to the notion of *economic viability* of financial institutions. Thus, for a financial institution's business model to be viable, it must generate nonnegative economic performance over time:

$$EP \geq 0$$

or equivalently,

$$R_A - R_L + F - E \geq C_C$$

This condition for economic viability is fairly intuitive: If an institution fails to deliver the required rate of return on capital on a consistent basis, its equity valuation multiple should experience a persistent decline, likely leading to an eventual liquidation.[3]

Static Business Models

The concept of economic performance illustrates that long-term profitability and survival of traditional financial businesses during the old regime passively depended on differential returns between assets and liabilities plus fees exceeding expenses and the cost of capital. Despite its simplicity, this observation has far-reaching implications. It allows us to examine the properties of traditional business models of financial institutions and the pressures they face in the changing world. Consider the following examples that further illustrate how traditional financial businesses generated profits during the old regime.

Commercial banks would originate loans (while paying special attention to the credit risk of the borrowers during the underwriting process), fund them with a combination of retail and wholesale liabilities, and "ride" the yield spread between assets and liabilities until maturity. Differential interest-rate and credit risks between assets and liabilities would not be managed across economic cycles, which means that the total economic return $(R_A - R_L)$ from this activity would be thought of as the nominal asset/liability spreads adjusted for realized credit losses and other impairments. Whenever the outlook on credit fundamentals would become negative, banks would tighten underwriting standards and shrink balance sheets. Throughout this process, while the total enterprise-wide risk would change proportionally with the size of balance sheets, the earnings' drivers described in the language of risk management would remain unchanged.

Other cases in point illustrate a similar *buy-and-hold* behavior in other financial sectors. Thus, strategic asset allocations ("policy portfolios") of defined benefit pension plans in the United States would remain largely unchanged for years and even decades at a time, typically consisting of a 65 percent allocation to equities, 30 percent allocation to fixed income, and 5 percent allocation to other asset classes. While some of the assets would be actively managed within fairly tight risk limits, the funding status (the differential fair value between assets and liabilities) would be largely determined by the underlying structural risk exposures to movements of equity and fixed-income markets.

In another example, portfolio businesses of government-sponsored enterprises (GSEs) in the United States would only grow when differences in expected returns between assets and liabilities (after hedging out interest rate risks) would be attractive. These residual A/L returns (in the case of GSEs represented by mortgage/agency option-adjusted spreads) would remain as is on balance sheets until maturity. Similar modi operandi generally applied to various activities of investment banks, insurance companies, central banks, and financial services firms as well as financial activities of non-financial corporations in the past. Table 2.1 illustrates the dominant

TABLE 2.1   Drivers of Economic Performance in a Static World

Institution	$R_A - R_L$	Fees
Depositories & Investment REITS	Loss-adjusted asset/liability spread (buy-and-hold, all fixed income)	Deposit account service charges, loan origination, servicing, and ATM fees, etc.
Insurers	Loss-adjusted asset/liability spread (buy-and-hold, mostly fixed income)	Surrender charges, management, and other misc. fees
Investment Banks	Loss-adjusted asset/liability spread (funding activities)	Bid/ask spreads, commissions, underwriting, and securitization fees
GSEs	Option-adjusted A/L spread (given typical hedging and debt management strategies)	Securitization fees
DB Pensions	Realized differential returns: equities vs. bonds (equity risk premium)	

components of economic performance for different types of financial institutions during the old regime.

Notice the following commonality among the examples presented in Table 2.1. In order to enhance economic performance, differential spreads between assets and liabilities as well as fees need to be increased by growing corresponding businesses. Meanwhile, expenses need to be minimized to the extent possible. While some market timing may be used in deciding when and how to expand or contract balance sheets, (a) the collection of risks underlying earnings and (b) composition of revenues across risk taking vis-à-vis fee-based activities both remain largely unchanged over time. This leads to the following conclusion: *With respect to the process of economic value creation, business models of financial institutions during the old regime can be characterized as static.*

In this context, the term *static* refers to the financial institutions' adherence to the traditional ways in which their balance sheets were deployed to fulfill chartered intermediation roles. Of particular importance in this discussion, *static* also emphasizes the *absence of dynamic and explicit risk-taking behavior and business model transformations* and is not to be confused with visionary M & A actions, customer service, client retention strategies, new product development, cross-selling, or expense management. In those areas, financial institutions have been far from static in the past.

Properties of Static Business Models

The old maxim from Chapter 1 about the nature of the job of a commercial banker—"borrow at 2 percent, lend at 6 percent, be on the golf course at 3 pm"—vividly expresses the old way of thinking about the task of economic value creation and is apropos to describing the properties of static business models as follows.

- Economic performance and viability are primarily determined by the level of fees as well as the differential returns between held-to-maturity assets and liabilities. During the old regime, fees and A/L spreads were relatively generous, affording the luxury of static behavior. In fact, the implication of the banker joke is that what an institution earns on its assets is so much larger than its cost of its liabilities that it is more than enough to cover expenses and produce a handsome return on capital.
- Systematic risk exposures (e.g., interest rates, credit spreads, mortgage prepayments, implied volatilities, equity risk premia) that underlie asset/liability spreads are not always understood even though they are direct consequences of the intermediation role of the financial institution. Since risks are not actively managed over time, executives do not

need to explicitly rely on macroeconomic and market views. The use of investment analyses in executive decisions is limited.

- The inherent cyclicality of unhedged underlying systematic risk factors—that correlates with expansions or contractions of the economy as a whole—often results in the cyclicality of accounting earnings as well as the latent economic performance. Fortunately, when the compensation (expected return per unit of risk) for traditional financial services is high, as was indeed the case during the old regime, there is more room for risk management mistakes.
- The use of advanced financial tools—including derivatives, securitization, debt management, and capital structure optimization—is usually confined to achieving business objectives as opposed to active risk-taking decisions.
- Due to the absence of dynamic risk-taking behavior, relatively stable business mix, and the limited use of derivatives and securitization:
  1. Charter-based regulation is adequate;
  2. Standard financial disclosures describe balance sheets, inherent risks, and future prospects of financial institutions reasonably well; and,
  3. Accounting earnings generally reflect economic performance over time, and, therefore, fair valuation is not required.
- Enterprise risk management (ERM) is a policing function primarily used to monitor risk limits and ensure compliance. ERM is not used to optimize balance sheets, enhance economic performance, or communicate with stakeholders.

Pillars of Decision Making During the Old Regime

In an environment where static business models produce adequate earnings due to high fees and generous asset/liability spreads while economic performance is reasonably approximated by accounting earnings, the main objectives of executives running traditional financial businesses can be described as follows.

- Create a robust business mix of asset/liability and fee-generating businesses through organic business development and M & A.
- Grow individual businesses through a variety of business- and customer-related activities. In this realm, financial executives typically work with investment bankers and consultants on such business aspects as increasing brand power, developing "champion" businesses, enhancing footprint and market share, designing effective cross-selling strategies, positioning in attractive underlying markets, and leveraging inherent competitive advantages.

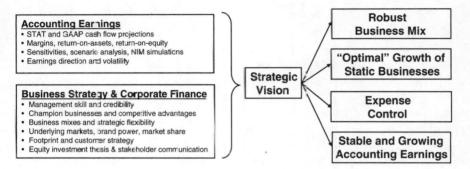

FIGURE 2.1 Pillars of Strategic Decision Making in the Static World

- Generate stable and growing accounting earnings.
- Control expenses.
- Preserve strategic flexibility.
- Achieve premium equity market valuation. An especially important aspect of strategic and investment banking discussions, this task involves a) analyzing the dominant business features of financial institutions and their business lines from the viewpoints of various stakeholders, b) examining the perceived management competency and credibility, and c) crafting deliberate communications with capital markets, rating agencies, and regulators.

I refer to this entire process—and the corresponding rich set of activities—as *business strategy and corporate finance.*

Given the nature of financial executives' objectives and activities discussed above, accounting earnings and business strategy combined with corporate finance constituted the two pillars of strategic decision making in the old regime, as shown in Figure 2.1.

This book will show that, as the task of economic value creation is transformed by the dynamic new world, the pillars of strategic decision making shown in Figure 2.1 must be expanded in order to enable the desirable evolutionary responses to modern challenges.

The Role of Risk Management

Properties of static business models help explain the disconnect between risk management and executive decision making often witnessed during the old regime. Consider a state of affairs in which economic performance is thought of in terms of differential asset/liability spreads and fees, while business decisions focus on maximizing accounting earnings of buy-and-hold businesses. In such a setting, risk management is destined to be a passive safety-and-soundness verification *after* major strategic decisions had been made. Moreover, advances in financial theory, analytics, and technology that lead to an increasingly rigorous understanding of complex portfolios and balance sheets may prove insufficient for elevating risk management to be a decision tool, as it has indeed been the case. For the mental divide between strategic decisions and risk management to disappear, risk taking must become explicitly linked to the process of economic value creation, with risk management becoming the very language of strategic decisions. Risk-focused regulation (Basel II and Solvency II) should contribute to the change of the existing mental paradigm somewhat. As always, however, the most effective catalyst of change is necessity, which leads us to the subject matter of the next sections—pressures on static business models brought about by the global forces of the dynamic new world.

Dominant Forces: The Future that Has Already Happened

Many best-selling business books on leadership and change discuss the necessity to identify and anticipate, in Peter Drucker's words, "the future that has already happened," emphasizing the need to evolve and respond to pressures with insight and decisive action. One of the best known examples of this genre is Spencer Johnson's *Who Moved My Cheese,* which is particularly relevant to the subject matter at hand. In the parable of mice and humans living in a maze, characters seek cheese for different reasons and respond differently after discovering that it is running out. The reader is led to a conclusion that while no single reaction may be inherently better than others, failure to adapt has a sad ending more often than not. This argues for the necessity to embrace change—as opposed to denying or resisting it.

During the Golden Age of financial intermediation, financial institutions enjoyed tamer competitive landscapes, significant informational advantages, lesser efficiency of financial markets, and higher compensation for risk-taking across asset classes. The combination of buy-and-hold asset/liability spreads and fees produced adequate earnings, affording financial institutions the luxury of maintaining static business models across economic cycles. In this section, I illustrate how the combination of global forces that came to the forefront during the time period affectionately dubbed by economists the Great Moderation (1985–present) has heightened the pressures on static business models across financial sectors. Understandably, the first response of many financial executives and investors to these changes was to hope that they were temporary and that the good old times would return. Given the nature of many of these forces described below, I view this as highly unlikely.

First, is the group of *secular* forces, which, by definition, are expected to influence the global financial system and financial institutions over very long time frames.

1. *Globalization of capital markets and financial services* as well as *their integration with real economies* are among the most important secular trends relevant to financial institutions. The total value of the financial services industry has risen by 60 percent between 1997 and 2007, reaching $6 trillion. Meanwhile, total revenues of financial services firms have reached $2.7 trillion, which equates to 7 percent of global GDP.[4] According to IMF data, since 1980 total trade in goods and services worldwide has increased at more than twice the rate of real GDP growth. The stock of international assets and liabilities has grown sharply in relation to GDP. Monthly net foreign purchases of U.S. assets went up more than tenfold between 1980 and 2007. Currency trading has become one of the fastest growing retail trading businesses, while emerging markets have turned into one of the fastest growing segments of financial markets. International operations of major financial institutions have expanded dramatically. Capital markets and financial institutions have begun playing a progressively more important role in the functioning of real economies. "Heavily controlled, segmented, and sleepy domestic financial systems have given way to a lightly regulated, open, and vibrant global financial system." Eventually, according to some estimates, securitization in the emerging market (EM) countries can potentially result in a multitrillion-dollar EM asset-backed securities market, with hundreds of millions of new consumers and homeowners benefiting from greater access to the global capital markets.[5] Figure 2.2 shows graphically the historical as well as projected growth of global financial services revenues from 1997 through 2017.

2. *Inflation targeting* and control by central banks around the world—coupled with globalization—are arguably responsible for the decline in both levels and variability of inflation, which are among the most distinguishing characteristics of this new period. As inflation declined significantly in many developed countries, this, in turn, led to lower interest rates and lower realized market volatility over prolonged periods of time. Figure 2.3 shows the dampened volatility of inflation, GDP, and interest rates over the past 25 years.

3. *Disintermediation* is the process of cutting out the middleman. In a retail setting, customers may bypass a wholesaler and buy directly from the manufacturer, thereby paying less. In the context of this book, disintermediation refers to the removal of financial institutions from the usual channels associated with the flows of funds and risks. Corporations, investors, and increasingly sophisticated consumers of financial

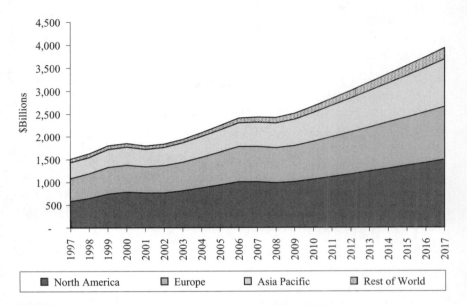

FIGURE 2.2 Global Financial Services' Revenues (1997–2017)
Source: From Oliver Wyman (2005), "The Future of Financial Services".

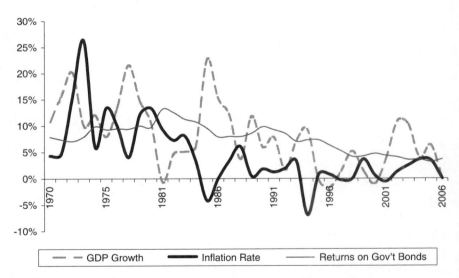

FIGURE 2.3 Global GDP, Inflation, and Interest Rages (1970–2006)
Source: From Mitchell (2003), OECD, Oliver Wyman Analysis.

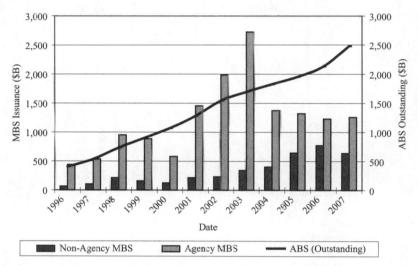

FIGURE 2.4 Mortgage-Backed and Asset Backed Securities (1996–2007)
Source: SIFMA.

products begin to deal with each other directly (e.g., via the Internet) or through new kinds of intermediaries instead of going through commercial banks or investment banks. Investors are granted easier access to the capital markets and a broader selection of service providers. The same applies to borrowers who gain access to the capital markets through securitization (Figure 2.4) as well as via new ways of issuing debt and equity. In general, disintermediation typically results in lower costs of products and services. Along with greater availability of financial information, disintermediation is responsible for the secular compression of the fees associated with basic financial services.[5]

4. *Greater availability of financial information* goes hand in hand with the process of financial disintermediation. The most up-to-date market and financial product data are no longer only available to institutional investors and financial institutions. Prices on financial instruments, loan rates, and insurance premiums—along with related fees and commissions—are obtainable virtually in real-time by anyone with an Internet connection. Securitization, increased competition, and financing alternatives have resulted in more efficient market- and risk-based pricing of financial products and services across the board, contributing to margin pressures faced by financial institutions.

5. *Alternative investment* vehicles—such as *hedge funds* and *private equity funds*—have dramatically affected the global capital flows, behavior of capital markets, business models of other financial institutions, and the overall leverage of the financial system. Alternative investments play a

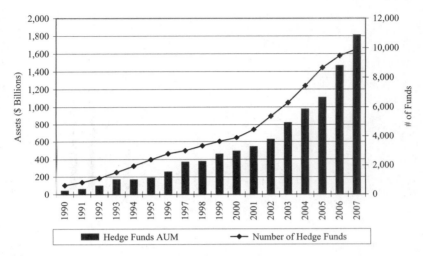

FIGURE 2.5 Hedge Funds Assets Under Management (1990–2007)

Source: HFR Industry Reports, © HRF, Inc., Q3 2007, www.hedgefundresearch.com.

very important role in this book. First, they are directly linked to principal investments—a component of the risk-based economic performance equation discussed in Chapter 3. Second, they have special relevance to the lessons learned from modern financial crises. Just think of the role of hedge funds in major market crises as well as of the profound impact of private equity activities on equity markets, high-yield markets, and collateralized loan obligations markets during certain time periods. Figures 2.5 and 2.6 show the dramatic growth in hedge funds, private equity funds, and real estate investment trusts in recent decades.

6. *Efficient financial markets*, as the Nobel Prize laureate William Sharpe puts it best in his *Investments*, result from a large number of investors believing that markets are *not* efficient and then attempting to deliver abnormal returns. While this premise is a source of an ongoing heated debate in both the financial industry and academia, Figure 2.7 simply illustrates the growth of aggregate assets under management of hedge funds that specifically focus on various forms of market "arbitrage," including relative value, fixed income, merger, and convertible arbitrage. Due to the greater availability of financial information, new financial markets that trade increasingly granular financial risks, use of computer trading technologies, and—most importantly—trillions of dollars in (often unconstrained) capital freely flowing around the world in search for returns, many market participants subscribe to the notion that *normal market environments* today are characterized by ever-greater financial market efficiency.

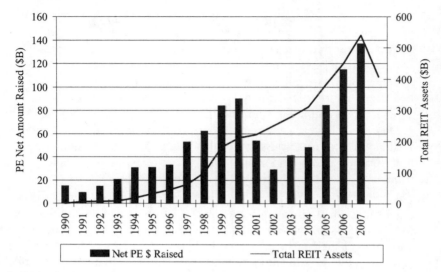

FIGURE 2.6 Private Equity Funds and REITs (1990–2007)

Source: Thomson Financial; SNL Financial.

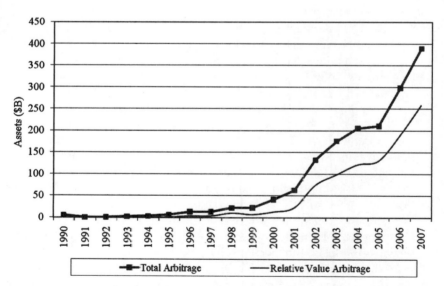

FIGURE 2.7 Assets of Hedge Funds that Focus on Arbitrage

Source: HFR Industry Reports, © HFR, Inc., Q3 2007,
www.hedgefundresearch.com.

7. *Financial deregulation* (i.e., liberalization) strives, among other things, to increase the efficiency of financial markets by eliminating "price controls, portfolio requirements, product restrictions, and barriers to entry" within a financial system. Additionally, liberalization may seek to "eliminate restrictions designed to insulate domestic financial service markets from international financial markets."[7] This effectively facilitates capital market globalization and provides financial institutions with greater flexibility in determining "optimal" business model mixes as well as the products and services that they offer to customers. Innovation, increased competition, and numerous economic benefits are often cited as the benefits of financial deregulation.

8. *The convergence* (blurring of the lines) between different financial businesses is a direct consequence of deregulation as well as the response of financial institutions to margin pressures on basic financial businesses and undiversified business mixes. Relevant examples of financial convergence include some modern financial institutions that are, in essence, hybrids of commercial banks and securities firms. Other financial institutions are hybrids of hedge funds, private equity firms, and real estate investment trusts (REITs). Financial conglomerates consisting of a commercial bank, an insurance company, a wealth management firm, and an investment bank also exist.

9. *Increasingly complex financial instruments* such as *derivatives and structured products* are an important (and permanent) feature of modern capital markets. Listed equity options are among the fastest growing instruments. Interest-rate derivatives, credit default swaps, and collateralized debt obligations have all experienced explosive growth. As shown in Figure 2.8, CDO issuance in the United States alone exceeded $400 billion in both 2006 and 2007 before coming to a halt during the subsequent crisis. The total notional outstanding of interest-rate derivatives grew from $75 trillion in 2001 to $388 trillion in 2007, according to the Bank For International Settlements. In special relevance to this book, complex financial products afford financial institutions and investors powerful ways of eliminating undesired risks as well as expressing investment views. It is through structured product and derivatives markets—by means of securitization, investing, and hedging—that business models of financial institutions can be drastically altered, with risks disseminated around the globe. These financial instruments are integral to the dynamic management of systematic risks as a means of economic value creation. On the flip side, lack of transparency and periodic illiquidity of these products can play an important role in the way that modern financial crises may unfold.

10. *Advances in technology, financial theory, analytics, and risk management* have played a critical role in facilitating disintermediation, capital market innovation, the *atomization* of risks, the growth of

Issuance Year	Ratings		Transactions		Issuance (Billion)	
	Issuance	Outstanding	Issuance	Outstanding	US	EUR
1984	14	0	14	0	$5.89	
1985	26	14	26	14	$1.96	
1986	61	41	61	41	$4.55	
1987	42	100	39	100	$2.30	
1988	38	141	37	138	$4.02	
1989	35	167	30	163	$4.06	
1990	22	188	22	180	$2.80	
1991	26	176	26	168	$3.23	
1992	39	189	39	181	$4.86	
1993	98	208	94	200	$5.89	
1994	6	298	6	287	$1.01	
1995	25	255	25	244	$4.95	
1996	23	277	21	266	$8.22	
1997	87	287	50	275	$32.53	EUR 0.20
1998	160	345	91	300	$57.63	EUR 4.49
1999	404	456	203	345	$58.92	EUR 11.14
2000	495	837	197	541	$70.96	EUR 16.94
2001	723	1276	278	698	$91.75	EUR 28.27
2002	1190	1954	436	952	$112.20	EUR 34.63
2003	1389	3020	727	1340	$78.31	EUR 28.76
2004	2885	4218	1833	1955	$141.47	EUR 233.65
2005	2967	6486	1622	3315	$304.58	EUR 192.24
2006	4395	8648	1883	4354	$434.34	EUR 83.48
2007	4138	12044	1743	5688	$425.33	EUR 78.52
ALL	19288		9503			

Issuance refers to the number of new ratings or transactions during the year.

Outstanding refers to the number of ratings or transactions at the beginning of the year.

AAA ratings from the same transaction are treated as a single rating in the calculation of this table.

Global CDO includes cash, synthetic and market value CDOs as well as leveraged funds.

FIGURE 2.8 Standard & Poor's Global CDO Issuance, 1984-2007

structured products, and the rise of alternative investments. The increasing power and declining cost of computer technology have resulted in the introduction of progressively more complex financial instruments, enabling the effective implementation of progressively complex hedging and investment strategies.

I refer to the *second group* of forces that brought the pressures faced by traditional financial businesses to the forefront during the Great Moderation as *period-specific*. While at this stage of the new dynamic order the permanence of these factors is unclear, their impact on the financial landscape of recent decades is noteworthy.

1. *Disinflation exporting* refers to a phenomenon whereby the abundance of low-cost labor in developing countries—combined with the liberalization of trade—has thus far limited inflation in developed countries. This happens because producers find it difficult to pass price increases onto the consumers in the face of global competition. Along with inflation targeting and globalization, it is disinflation exporting that is believed to have led to a decline in both realized inflation and its variability over time, which, in turn, resulted in a low-return environment early in the twenty-first century.

2. *The global savings glut* represents a confluence of forces behind a significant increase in the global supply of savings. Among these factors are such demographic phenomena as an increase in the number of retirees in proportion to workers in the developed countries as well as changes in the global capital flows that facilitated the transition of many developing countries from net borrowers to net lenders.

3. *Bretton Woods* was the international monetary system between 1945 and 1971 in which the exchange rates at which foreign governments and central banks could freely convert U.S. dollars into gold were fixed.[8] Its modern reincarnation—*Bretton Woods II*—refers to the regime in which several countries, mostly in Asia and the Middle East, have adopted currency exchange rates that are pegged to the U.S. dollar. In most notable cases, the level at which these currencies had been pegged has resulted in a growing trade imbalance (deficit on the part of the United States). This, in turn, has led to a dramatic accumulation of foreign exchange reserves by the developing countries that were "recycled" (invested in securities) back into the United States, compressing investment returns during certain notable time periods. Figure 2.9 illustrates the evolution of cumulative net capital inflows in the United States and the corresponding foreign exchange reserves buildup in China and Brazil in recent decades. The persistent decline in the value of U.S. dollar around the time when this book is being written makes the potential of Bretton Woods II—and the very status of the dollar as the dominant reserve currency—uncertain.

No discussion on macroeconomic and market environments would be complete without the *third group* of the *cyclical* forces. While the Great Moderation spanned multiple economic cycles, cyclical forces at times exacerbated the pressures on traditional financial businesses brought about by secular and period-specific forces. For example, *global economic expansion; favorable corporate and consumer credit fundamentals* that facilitated borrowing; *low default rates, strong housing markets, and robust demand for commodities* all played an important role in exacerbating the vicious

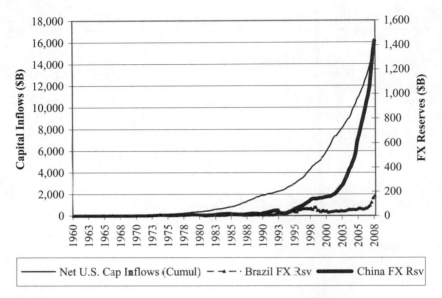

FIGURE 2.9 Foreign Exchange Reserves and Capital Flows (1960-2008)
Source: Haver Analytics, FRB.

circle of risk taking and leverage in a prelude to some notable financial dislocations.

Pressures on Static Business Models

The net impact of these forces on major financial sectors is illustrated in Table 2.2. Margins (or asset/liability spreads), underwriting fees, and trading commissions have all experienced a systematic and arguably secular compression in recent decades. Anecdotal evidence suggests that the compensation for other basic financial intermediation activities—loan origination fees, bid/ask spreads in normal market environments, clearing activities, and asset management fees for large institutional mandates and mutual funds—has declined as well (not shown).[9]

Let us now look closely at how the developments described in Table 2.2 affected each major financial sector.

Pressures on Commercial Banks

Margin pressures faced by commercial banks with traditional business models serve as a telling example of the ongoing changes in the world of finance. By definition, bank net interest margins (NIMs), depicted in the first line on Table 2.2, represent the accounting analog of the differential return between

TABLE 2.2   Reduction in Compensation for Basic Financial Services and Investments

Institutional Example	Economic Performance Driver	Past Level	Current Level or Future Expectations	Difference
Depositories	Net Interest Margin[1]	4.2% (1992)	3.4% (2007)	−25%
Insurers	Net Interest Yield[2]	7.01 (1997)	5.48 (2007)	−22%
Brokers	Commissions-Equities (per share)[3]	$0.25 (1980)	0.01–0.5 (2007)	−88%
Investment Banks	Representative Debenture Underwriting Fees[4]	50–85 bps (1997)	12–20 bps (2007)	−76%
Pensions	Equity Risk Premium[5]	5% (avg. 1925–2000)	0.5–3% (expectation)	−55%

Sources: FDIC[1]; SNL Financial[2]; Sanford Bernstein LLC[3]; Bloomberg[4]; Arnott and Berstein (2002) and Siegel (1999)[5].

assets and liabilities $(R_A - R_L)$. Observing the NIM evolution of commercial banks over the past 15 years in Figure 2.10, first note the cyclicality of NIMs that is not at all surprising: The unhedged borrow short/lend long balance sheet exposure (yield curve carry trade) is the essence of the traditional depository business of taking in deposits and investing the proceeds in longer-maturity loans or securities. Because of the inherent yield curve risk, margins tend to improve in periods of steep yield curves and get hurt when yield curves flatten or invert. Second, the overall margin compression trend appears self-evident: It can be attributed to both the relative rise in the cost of liabilities and a relative decline in return on assets, each driven by a different set of forces described in the previous section. Thus, higher liability costs are driven by disintermediation, higher competition, and greater availability of financial information. On the other hand, returns on assets are influenced by a multitude of forces ranging from inflation targeting and securitization to currency regimes and cyclical factors. It is important to emphasize that, in response to margin pressures, many commercial banks have already begun to address the limitations of static business models by behaving more dynamically. As I discuss later in this book, in addition to growing fee-based businesses, they are managing systematic risks more proactively.

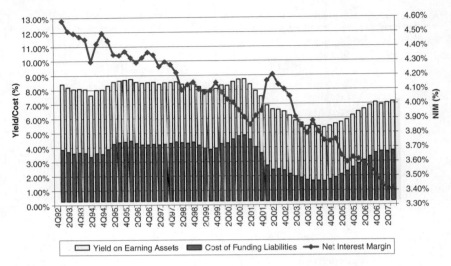

FIGURE 2.10 Net Interest Margin Trends of Large U.S. Commercial Banks
Source: FDIC.

Thus, the NIM compression in Figure 2.10 likely *understates* the actual pressures facing purely static depository business models, as seen from the following comparison. While NIMs of commercial banks declined by about 10 percent between 2001 and 2007, their returns on assets (RoAs) remained generally unchanged due to the growth of fee-based businesses, as shown in Figure 4.5. During the same time period, NIMs and returns on average assets of credit unions—whose business models are much more static and constrained than those of commercial banks—declined by 19 percent and 40 percent, respectively.[10]

Pressures on Life Insurance Companies

The perils of failing to adjust to the changing market environment by holding onto static business models are vividly illustrated by the experience of the U.S. life insurance industry early in the twenty-first century. In 2000, when interest rates started to decline while competitive pressures continued to increase, most insurers did not lower expectations of differential returns between assets and liabilities to reflect the changing realities. More specifically, book yield (accounting return) targets of portfolios corresponding to level-premium products remained unchanged, and the same unrealistic assumptions were simultaneously used in pricing new insurance products. To achieve required levels of A/L returns and maintain fee income from new products during the decline in interest rates, insurers invested in progressively riskier credit and mortgage-backed securities on the asset side

TABLE 2.3   Short Options Embedded in Insurance Liabilities

Product Type	Policy Types	Product Feature	Embedded Short Option
Risk	Term Life Disability, Long-Term, and Cancer Care	Option to renew a policy at guaranteed premiums	Call on the value of future benefit payments
Investment	Fixed and Variable Annuities	Right to deposit additional premiums into existing fixed rate deferred annuity	Call on the value of future annuity payments
		Withdrawal option and various guaranteed death and income benefits	Put on the value of the policy
		Guaranteed min return with appreciation potential	Interest rate floor
Hybrid	Permanent, Whole, and Variable Life	Option to convert the policy to cash	Put on the value of the policy
		Option to borrow cash against the policy at predetermined interest rates	Series of puts on fixed rate bonds

Note. From Gilles et al., Long -term economic and market trends and their implications for asset/liability management of insurance companies. *Journal of Risk Finance,* Winter 2003.

and shorted an increasing quantity of often-mispriced options on the liability side (Table 2.3). Additionally, reinvestment risk was not explicitly managed, and the overall increase in exposures to systematic risks (interest rates, prepayments, credit, and volatility risks) was not always understood.

Subsequently, as the U.S. economy slipped into the recession in 2001, interest rates declined, equity markets sold off, credit losses increased, and prepayments rose, causing what Moody's described as "significant damage to industry's capital and earnings,"[11] as revealed in Figure 2.11. In 2001–2002, realized losses of 20 top life insurers amounted to almost $11 billion, with average return on assets dropping to below 2 percent in 2002.

Pressures on Pension Plans

Echoing the insurance example, the experience of U.S. defined-benefit pension plans during the first decade of the twenty-first century was equally troublesome—and also related to structural risk exposures underlying static

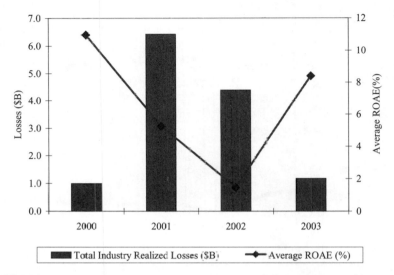

FIGURE 2.11 Representative 20 Large U.S. Life Insurers' ROAE and Realized Losses
Sources: SNL Financial.

business models. Historically, assets of defined-benefit pension plans were heavily skewed toward equities, with typical strategic asset allocations comprised of 65 percent equities, 30 percent fixed income, and 5 percent in other asset classes. This was contrary to the fixed-income nature of their liabilities that are, in essence, streams of cash flows subject to various uncertainties (e.g., inflation, mortality). These liabilities are not highly correlated with equity markets.

Due to the nature of their strategic asset allocations, static business models, and lack of asset/liability management sophistication, defined-benefit pension plans have historically been structurally long equity markets and short fixed-income markets. Because of this reliance on the differential returns between equities and fixed income, we refer to the systematic risk factor underlying the pension's business model as *equity risk premium* throughout this book.

Not surprisingly, a simultaneous drop in equity prices and a decline in interest rates decrease the market value of pension assets and increase the present value of pension liabilities, resulting in significant funding shortfalls. Figure 2.12 shows the performance of a hypothetical static defined-benefit pension plan between 2000 and 2007. During that time, according to Ryan ALM, Inc., assets of a plan that adhered to a static asset allocation (5% Ryan Cash Index, 30% Lehman Aggregate, 60% S&P 500, 5% EAFE) grew by 33 percent, while its liabilities (modeled as the Ryan Liability Benchmark) grew by 110 percent. Thus, due to asset/liability

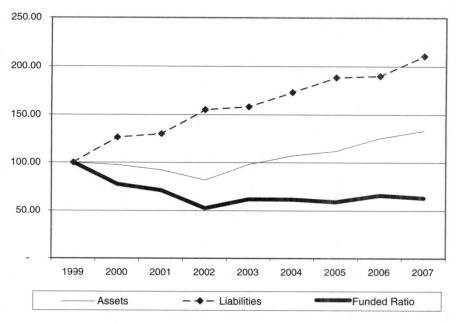

FIGURE 2.12 Funded Status of a Hypothetical DB Pension Plan (1999–2007)
Source: Ryan ALM, Inc.

mismatches involving systematic risks, a pension plan with a static business model that was fully funded in 1999 would have been underfunded by about 37 percent in 2007. By implication, a pension plan that was overfunded by 30 percent in 1999 would have been underfunded by 20 percent in 2007 (funded ratios of 130 percent and 80 percent, respectively). The latter case is generally consistent with the actual experience of pension plans in the United States, as seen from the distribution of funded statuses of public pensions in Figure 2.13. In general, it is fair to say that business models of defined-benefit pensions plans have remained static over the recent decades, with problems stemming primarily from structural A/L mismatches.

With pension-funded ratios being completely at the mercy of movements of fixed income and equity markets, unhedged structural risk exposures and inherent funding status volatility were duly noted by sponsors and regulators alike. Liability-driven investing and progressively larger allocations to alternative investments are among the initiatives directed at changing the static nature of pensions' business models and their structural exposures to systematic risks. Both are generally consistent with the desirable evolutionary responses advocated in this book.

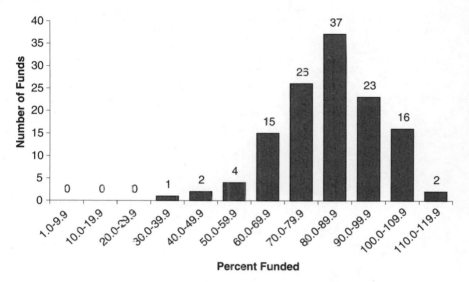

FIGURE 2.13 Funded Ratios of Largest State and Local DB Pension Plans (2007)
Source: United States Government Accountability Office.

Pressures on Securities Firms, Money Center Banks, and Monoline Insurers

The low-return environment of 2003–2006—coupled with ongoing secular margin pressures—resulted in many securities firms, money center banks, insurance companies, and other financial institutions actively searching for new sources of revenues. Seemingly ignoring the lessons learned from life insurers earlier in the decade, many financial firms with static business models ended up generating these additional revenues by taking on more risk, including via larger exposures to highly complex financial instruments as collateralized debt obligations (CDOs), leveraged loans, and lower-credit-quality mortgage-backed securities. These instruments were held either directly on balance sheets or inside of facilities used to warehouse loans, securitize them, and sell securities to investors. Importantly, as became apparent after the fact, the increase in systematic risk exposures was not always understood and not actively managed.

When the housing market bubble started to deflate in 2007, delinquencies started to increase significantly across prime, Alt-A, and subprime mortgage loans, especially those originated in 2006 and 2007. For example, by early 2008, 60 ± day delinquencies on 12- to 16-month-old subprime pools reached as high as 17 percent, as compared to just 4 percent on the 2003 vintage loans. Meanwhile, securitization markets froze, and credit spreads widened significantly, sending ripple effects across global financial

TABLE 2.4   Top-Ten Write Downs by Financial Sector (Q3 & Q4 2007)

Banks & Securities Firms	Write Downs ($B)	Capital Raised ($B)	Insurance Companies	Write Downs ($B)	Capital Raised ($B)
Citigroup	22.8	25.9	AIG	7.7	—
Merrill Lynch	22.0	12.8	Ambac	6.2	1.5
UBS	18.1	9.8	MBIA	2.7	1.8
HSBC	17.2	—	MGIC	2.4	0.8
Morgan Stanley	11.9	5	Ntixis	1.9	—
Bank of America	8.0	12	ACA	1.1	—
JPMorgan Chase	5.2	—	SwissRe	0.9	1.6
Credit Agricole	5.2	—	PMI	0.8	—
Credit Suisse	4.8	—	AGC	0.5	0.6
Deutsche Bank	3.2	—	FSA	0.5	0.5
Total	**121.2**	**65.5**		**24.6**	**6.7**

Note: From respective companies' press releases, as of April 1, 2008.

markets. As extensive write downs were taken by a wide range of financial institutions, as shown in Table 2.4, capital ratios became strained and the capital had to be raised at very expensive levels in the most inopportune time—during a market dislocation. Interestingly, a large portion of these newly issued capital securities were consumed by sovereign wealth funds—including Abu Dhabi Investment Authority, Kuwait Investment Authority, Korea Investment Corporation, Singapore's Tamasek Holdings, and China Investment Corporation—in a testament to the globalization of capital markets and the behavioral change on the part of these increasingly influential market participants.

Meanwhile, monoline insurance companies were also faced with related write downs stemming from concentrated risks inherent in credit-wrap insurance of CDOs and mortgage-backed securities. Significant volatility and decline in equity valuations across financial sectors followed, as shown in Figure 2.14.

The economic performance equation presented earlier in this chapter illuminates the limitations of static business models, shedding light on the problematic institutional experiences early in the twenty-first century, which are summarized in Table 2.5. Once a common framework is applied to different financial sectors, seemingly different industry circumstances and nuances become mostly irrelevant, revealing the universality of challenges and striking similarity of behaviors. The common themes are straightforward. First, thinking about economic value creation in terms of differential returns between assets and liabilities is dangerous because the nature and magnitude of underlying financial risks is obscured. Second, institutions with

FIGURE 2.14 Performance of Financial Stocks (2003–April 2008)

Source: From Bloomberg, LP. Monoline index is weighted by the beginning-of-period capitalization.

static business models tend to respond to margin pressures and low-return environments by taking on increasing amounts of risks—often without even knowing it!

The Need for a New Paradigm

A colleague once compared the task of navigating the ongoing financial revolution to the sport called *orienteering*, where competitors use a map and compass to race their way through unfamiliar territory.[12] With one caveat: The race is taking place in an area that is undergoing a tectonic shift, which causes the maps to become periodically outdated and participants periodically lost. An observer of financial markets in recent years can relate to the metaphor. The increased uncertainty and complexity of both capital markets and financial institutions have led to extreme informational overload and rampant speculation. Market sentiments would change abruptly and frequently, with oxymoronic news headlines informing everyone of sudden "squalls" upsetting the prevailing "structured" thinking.[13] Given the

TABLE 2.5   Losses Stemming from Pressures on Static Business Models

Financial Sector	Pressures on Static Business Models	Magnitude
Line Insurers[1]	Realized losses due to excessive risk-taking in response to secular pressures and a low-return environment	−$11B (2002–2003)
DB Pensions[2]	Decline in funding status due to mismatched A/L risks	−50% (1999–2007)
Securities Firms Commercial Banks Insurers[3]	Significant write downs due to excessive risk-taking in response to secular pressures and a low-return environment	−$200B+ (2007–2008)

Note. From SNL Financial; Ryan ALM, Inc. & U.S. Govt Accountability Office; Companies' Releases 2007–2008 writedown data is as of April 1, 2008.

sheer number of forces at play, depictions of the new reality became very fragmented. The financial press became filled with complex terms such as: carry trades, financial convergence, disintermediation, margin compression, low-return environment, marking-to-model, Level III assets, global savings glut, alpha/beta separation, global diffusion of financial risks, liability-driven investing, and risk-focused regulation. They represented descriptions of, or responses to, a particular aspect of the evolutionary change but offered little normative value overall. At times, as noted by a *New York Times* article, "market players [would] seem truly horrified—because they've suddenly realized that they don't understand the complex financial system they created."[14]

In the language of this book, pressures on traditional financial businesses—that used to be so successful during the old regime—intensified dramatically during the Great Moderation, affecting the behavior of financial markets and, accordingly, the state of mind of their participants. The viability of static business models became increasingly in doubt, forcing financial institutions to start exploring new forms of economic value creation. Yet an updated lens through which to view the changed reality remained illusive.

In the next chapter, I lay out the groundwork for changing the old way of thinking about economic performance by turning the accounting-earnings-inspired formula reflective of the old regime into a new risk-based expression. This, in turn, will enable us to explore dynamic risk taking, business model transformations, and other desirable evolutionary responses to modern-day challenges.

CHAPTER 3

The Dynamic New World

Risk-Based Economic Performance

In response to pressures on static financial businesses brought about by a multitude of global forces, financial institutions must redefine the role of dynamism in economic value creation. In this regard, measurement and interpretation of economic performance should change accordingly in order to reflect the new realities. In this section, I develop the concept of *risk-based economic performance*, thus setting the stage for a discussion of tools and strategies that enable financial executives to cope with modern-day challenges. Without any loss of understanding on how this new concept can be applied, the nontechnical reader can skip the analytical derivation that follows and proceed directly to the definition of the risk-based economic performance equation on page 67 and the subsequent discussion of its various components.

Let us return to the now-familiar economic performance equation that describes how financial institutions used to create economic value during the static old regime:

$$EP = R_A - R_L + F - E - C_C$$

where R_A and R_L are total economic returns on assets and liabilities; F and E are fees and expenses; and C_C is the cost of the firm's capital—all presented in terms of return-on-assets.

Before we proceed, let me remind the readers of the following features of static business models—and the corresponding ways of thinking—revealed through this equation in the previous chapter. First, presenting economic performance in terms of differential returns between assets and liabilities—and managing financial institutions accordingly—obscures underlying risks. Second, economic performance of static business models is at the mercy of external environments: If returns between assets and liabilities decline, financial institutions often respond to margin pressures by increasing leverage and engaging in various other forms of risk taking, the extent of which may not always be understood. Third, due to the inherent cyclicality of systematic risks, economic performance may exhibit cyclical behavior as well. How can we address the limitations of the old mental paradigms and corresponding practices?

As discussed in detail in Appendix A, we start by rewriting the old-regime economic performance equation as follows:

$$EP = \frac{A \cdot r_A - L \cdot r_L + \$F - \$E - C \cdot r_C}{A}$$

where r_A, r_L, and r_C are rates of return on assets, liabilities, and capital, respectively; $\$F$ and $\$E$ are fees and expenses in dollar terms; A and L are market values of assets and liabilities, respectively, and C is the *shareholders' equity* that simply equals to the difference between assets and liabilities. Note that in this equation, shareholders' equity represents the total capital of the firm, which is done for the sake of simplicity and without loss of generality: While the modern view of the firm's total capital involves hybrid capital instruments and convertible bonds in addition to preferred and common equity securities, this fact is not germane to the mathematical derivation at hand.

Thanks to modern financial theory, the risks hidden inside of different components of the economic performance equation can be unmasked. Thus, in order to make the concept of economic performance more relevant to institutional challenges and practices in a dynamic new world, let us express rates of returns corresponding to assets and liabilities using the following decompositions:

$$r_A = r_f + a_A + \sum b_{A;i} \cdot (r_{F;i} - r_f) + \varepsilon_A$$
$$r_L = r_f + a_L + \sum b_{L;i} \cdot (r_{F;i} - r_f) + \varepsilon_L$$

where r_f is a risk-free rate, a's are expected market-neutral excess returns, b's are factor loadings corresponding to *systematic* risk factors, $(r_{f;i} - r_f)$ are risk premia associated with systematic risk factors, and ε's are random errors that are uncorrelated with other terms.

In a deliberately less detailed fashion, let us separate the rate of return (r_C) corresponding to the cost of capital into the risk-free rate (r_f) and excess return ($r_{C;EX}$) components as follows:

$$r_C = r_f + r_{C;EX}$$

Following the substitution of these expressions for rates of return on assets, liabilities, and capital into the original equation, a sequence of mathematical simplifications presented in Appendix A helps us arrive at the following expression for economic performance:

$$EP = \alpha_A - \frac{L}{A}\alpha_L + \sum \left(b_{A;i} - \frac{L}{A} \cdot b_{L;i} \right) \cdot (r_{F;i} - r_f) + F - E - \frac{C}{A}r_{C;EX}$$

where α's are market-neutral excess returns for assets and liabilities.

For reasons that will be explained momentarily, let us switch the order of terms corresponding to α_A and α_L and adopt the following notations:

New	Previous	Definition
α_{ARB}	$-\frac{L}{A}a_L$	Benefits of persistently submarket funding, if any
α_{PI}	a_A	Market-neutral returns from principal investment activities
β_i	$b_{A;i} - \frac{L}{A}b_{L;i}$	Active exposures to systematic risks ("factor loadings")
RP_i	$r_{F\,i} - r_f$	Risk premia corresponding to systematic risk factors
C_C	$\frac{C}{A}r_{C;EX}$	Cost of capital in excess of the risk-free rate

Thus, we have arrived at the expression that is a basic key to understanding modern financial institutions and related financial market phenomena:

Risk-Based Economic Performance Equation

$$EP = \alpha_{ARB} + \alpha_{PI} + \sum \beta_i \cdot RP_i + F - E - C_C$$

The verbal definition of the risk-based economic performance equation is as follows

Economic performance in the dynamic new world is generated through balance sheet arbitrage α_{Arb}, principal investment activities α_{PI}, exposures to systematic risks $\sum \beta_i \cdot RP_i$, fee-based businesses F, cost-control E, and minimization of the cost of capital C_C.

I should note that this equation also applies exactly in its present form to economic performance from financial activities of non-financial corporations—the subject that will be briefly addressed later in the book. Last, reduced-form versions of this equation are undoubtedly familiar to the readers in the context of investment performance generated by asset managers:

Benchmarked asset manager: $EP = \alpha + \sum \beta_{\overline{K};i} \cdot RP_i - E$

Absolute return asset manager: $EP = r_f + \alpha + \sum \beta_i \cdot RP_i - E$

In the previous expressions, α's are market-neutral excess returns and E's are a combination of operating expenses and money management fees.

In the case of absolute return money managers, β_i represents absolute factor loadings. In the case of benchmarked money managers, $\beta_{R,i}$ represents relative factor loadings of portfolios against their benchmarks.

The risk-based economic performance equation describes the process of value creation in terms of conceptually different risk-taking and fee-generating activities, which I refer to as *risk-based business models*. Thus, in essence, this book introduces the most straightforward set of risk-based business models: balance sheet arbitrage, principal investments, systematic risks, and fees. More elaborate classifications of risk-based business models can be developed, analyzed, and linked to perspectives on financial intermediation, as discussed in Ho-Lee-Tilman's *The Risk Paradigm*. Similar to how advances in risk management lead to the identification and analysis of progressively specific dimensions of risks, the same is true with respect to risk-based business models.

As repeatedly emphasized throughout this book, capital markets have become increasingly embedded in the functioning of real economies as well as lives of consumers, financial institutions, governments, and corporations. In this regard, external environments greatly influence the process of economic value creation by financial institutions. Next, let us look more closely at the components of risk-based economic performance and discuss them in the context of the dominant macroeconomic and financial market phenomena.

Balance Sheet Arbitrage (α_{ARB})

The ability of some financial institutions to borrow funds at what can be described as submarket levels is obviously a rare and very desirable source of revenue in the era of highly efficient capital markets. While the term *balance sheet arbitrage* may offend finance purists, it simply alludes to institutional features (e.g., the charter or the nature of the business model) that enable financial institutions to generate nonsystematic returns on the liability side of the balance sheet without taking on significant corresponding risk exposures. Common examples of balance sheet arbitrage include funding advantages of Government Sponsored Enterprises (GSEs) vis-à-vis other financial institutions of similar creditworthiness as well as the differences between retail liabilities of depository institutions and their wholesale funding rates. Sometimes, balance sheet arbitrage is passed along by financial institutions that enjoy it to those less fortunate: For instance, Federal Home Loan Banks in the United States can pass a portion of their own balance sheet arbitrage to their members, with both parties sharing the profits. The fact that submarket funding contributes positively to economic performance explains the notational sign change $\alpha_{ARB} = -\alpha_L$ in the previous section.

While the funding advantage of GSEs appears to be in the cards for the foreseeable future given the political realities, balance sheet arbitrage enjoyed by depository institutions has experienced increasing pressures due to disintermediation, wider availability of financial information, greater capital market efficiency, and other secular trends. To understand the connection between this component of economic performance and external environments, first note that retail deposits of commercial banks are characterized by (a) funding levels that are substantially lower than wholesale borrowing rates as well as (b) relatively low and fairly asymmetric sensitivity to changes in interest rates. Via financial modeling, these two features can be analyzed and properly allocated between appropriate components of economic performance: balance sheet arbitrage and systematic risks. Not surprisingly, as pressures facing traditional financial businesses emerged toward the end of the Golden Age, the competition for retail deposits of commercial banks intensified, with the cumulative average growth rate (CAGR) of U.S. commercial bank branches (1.71%) significantly outpacing the U.S. population's CAGR (1.15%) between 1990 and 2006. As a net result, the relative costs of liabilities and their sensitivity to changes in interest rates both increased. Thus, during the 1994 to 1995 Fed tightening cycle, deposit rates went up on average by 100 basis points (bps) during a 300 bp increase in the Fed Funds rates (beta of 0.3). However, during the 2004 to 2006 tightening cycle, deposit rates increased by almost 200 bps during a 425 bp increase in the Fed Funds rates (beta of almost 0.5). The compression of the balance sheet arbitrage component of the economic performance equation helps explain a portion of margin pressures faced by traditional commercial banking businesses (Figure 2.2). Given the secular nature of many of the forces at play, further compression of the balance sheet arbitrage component of economic performance is likely, which should translate into continuing margin pressures.

Financial institutions work hard to preserve and enhance balance sheet arbitrage through a variety of business strategies and corporate finance activities. Meanwhile, equity market valuations of financial institutions may implicitly reflect, among other things, investor perceptions of a sustainability of submarket funding advantages as well as their contribution to the overall economic performance.

Principal Investments (α_{PI})

In response to the vulnerability of static business models and the need to supplement "core" earnings with nontraditional sources of revenues, active risk taking is playing an increasingly important role in the lives of modern financial institutions. In particular, principal investments—putting the firm's capital to work through a variety of investment activities and vehicles—represent one of the most common institutional reactions to across-the-board margin pressures. I define the principal investment component of the economic performance equation as a conglomeration of risk-taking activities of financial institutions whose returns are uncorrelated with systematic risks. Portfolios of private equity and venture capital investments, collections of proprietary trading desks, stakes or investments in hedge funds, and idiosyncratic risks of investments and loan portfolios are all placed under the umbrella of market-neutral principal investments. In contrast, returns generated by activities that entail exposures to *systematic risks* are excluded from this component of economic performance and are discussed in the next section.

The distinction between what I define as principal investment activities vis-à-vis systematic risk taking on an enterprise-wide level (*both of which put the firm's own capital at risk*) is important from both analytical and organizational perspectives. Financial theory instructs us that nonsystematic risks can be reduced via diversification—which is exactly the spirit in which financial institutions and institutional investors manage their portfolios of principal investments. In this regard, similar to the case of static business models, risk management is used to set risk limits beforehand and then measure and control exposures once business and investment decisions have been made. Needless to say, drawing the line between various real-world risk-taking activities can be nontrivial. For instance, certain supposedly market-neutral principal investment activities (like investments in hedge funds) may generate returns through market timing of systematic risks, while public equity stakes in foreign institutions often have both idiosyncratic and systematic components. In a way that is generally consistent with institutional practices, I have assumed that a portfolio of principal investment activities does not contain *structural* systematic risk exposures over time. This enables us to appropriately distinguish conceptually different activities and organizational structures within modern financial institutions.

In cases where the assumption that principal investment activities contain no structural systematic risk exposures proves incorrect, management of these systematic risks embedded in principal investments must become a part of a separate enterprise-wide process discussed in the next section. In fact, taking views on systematic risks requires an entirely different organizational setup, executive skills, analytical tools, and decision-making processes, with risk management playing a very different role. The failure to recognize the distinction between these different forms of risk taking can lead to a sad ending, as illustrated by notable news headlines at the time when this book was written. Thus, during certain market environments, a combination of alternative investments roaming about the world in search for performance and greater market efficiency may make the delivery of pure investment alpha very challenging.[1] As a result, hedge funds and proprietary trading desks may begin to derive an increasingly larger proportion of returns from systematic risks. This, in turn, can change the nature of their economic value creation and make diversification ineffective as the risk-management tool. This scenario must be explicitly addressed by firms that allocate capital to proprietary trading desks and by entities that make investments in hedge funds.

Making market-neutral principal investments a meaningful part of an institution's business model requires considerable organizational changes and entails significant risks, complexity, as well as—from the viewpoint of external stakeholders—lack of transparency and predictability.

Systematic Risk Exposures ($\sum \beta_i \cdot RP_i$)

In the world where traditional intermediation fees are experiencing a secular decline and balance sheet arbitrage is a rare and very valuable business feature, the shift toward economic value creation through active and dynamic risk taking should not come as a surprise. In addition to market-neutral principal investments, active management of *systematic risks* on financial institutions' balance sheets (commonly described in the money management community as *market timing* or *active beta investing*) is playing an increasingly important role in the process of economic value creation. Examples of systematic risks include interest rates, credit spreads, mortgage prepayments, implied volatilities, currencies, commodities, and equity indices. As a reminder, according to my adopted convention, while market-neutral principal investments may employ active beta investing, they are assumed to contain no *structural* systematic risk exposures over time.

The term $\sum \beta_i \cdot P_i$ in the economic performance equation encompasses all systematic risks embedded in balance sheets of financial institutions or institutional investment portfolios. In this setting, economic performance generated by systematic risk factors can be represented as the product of the active asset/liability mismatches or factor loadings $\beta_i = \beta_{A;i} - \beta_{L;i}$ and the corresponding risk premia $RP_i = (r_{F;i} - r_f)$. Note that while exposures to systematic risks in the economic performance equation are depicted as linear $\sum \beta_i \cdot P_i$ in a way that is consistent with classic financial constructs[2], this is done solely for the sake of simplicity of exposition and without loss of generality. In reality, this component of economic performance can encompass all types of exposures to systematic risk factors, both linear and nonlinear, and appropriate financial models can be used to measure expected economic returns without relying on the linearity assumption. Importantly, various options written by modern financial institutions and institutional investors reside inside this component of economic performance.

I naturally assume here that financial institutions have the analytical ability to measure the differential risk exposures (or factor loadings) between their assets and liabilities, which is obviously a highly nontrivial exercise in real life. It typically starts with the task of using financial models to represent liabilities as replicating portfolios of capital market instruments.[3] As an oversimplified illustration, consider a stylized defined benefit pension plan where 100 percent of assets are invested in the S & P 500 index. In order to understand the nature of its liabilities, actuarial assumptions can be used to project liability cash flows across scenarios and through time. Subsequently, hedging techniques can be used to construct a portfolio of fixed-income securities that most closely replicates these cash flows. Assume, for instance, that a pension plan's liabilities are akin to those of a 30-year bond. In this case, the systematic risk component of the economic performance equation can be defined in two equivalent ways: (a) having two risk factors, S & P 500 and a 30-year bond yield, or (b) having one risk factor, which is the difference between the returns on S & P 500 and a 30-year bond ($r_{S\&P\ 500} - r_{30\text{-}yr}$), which is typically referred to as the *equity risk premium relative to long-maturity interest rates*. In a more complex setting, consider the task of mapping retail deposits of commercial banks onto systematic risk factors—an exercise that relies on a great deal of subjective judgment and numerous assumptions. As mentioned before, retail bank deposits are characterized by persistently below-market funding levels as well as lagging and asymmetric sensitivity to changes in interest rates. For instance, deposit rates may change by 20 to 50 bps for every 100 bp move in short interest rates, with greater sensitivity observed in the declining interest rate environments. This behavior can be properly analyzed using financial models, with expected returns allocated between balance sheet arbitrage and systematic risk components of the economic performance equation.[4]

We are now ready to discuss the evolutionary implications of the risk-based economic performance equation and, in particular, its systematic risk component. Recall the discussion on the pressures faced by traditional financial businesses with static business models early in the twenty-first century presented in Chapter 2. While the fee compression was evident and understandable in the context of global forces at play, the identification of the exact sources of margin compression was challenging due to the old way of thinking about economic performance. Decomposing differential returns between assets and liabilities into various risk-based components as per the economic performance equation sheds light on the matter, leading to the following observation:

Earnings pressures facing traditional financial businesses become particularly severe if the secular compression in compensation for simple financial intermediation activities (fees and balance sheet arbitrage) happens to coincide with a decline in risk premia across asset classes.

In a very telling example, due to a simultaneous impact of secular, period-specific, and cyclical forces, the following three components of economic performance relevant to the traditional financial businesses—balance sheet arbitrage, fees, and compensation for bearing systematic risks—all came under pressure during certain parts of the Great Moderation (e.g., 2003–2006, Figure 3.1). This provides the most direct explanation of the earnings pressures faced by static business models and the vicious circles of leverage and risk taking that followed. In response to margin pressures, financial institutions attempt to minimize expenses and cost of capital to the extent possible. When this proves insufficient, the fight for balance sheet arbitrage intensifies, explicit leverage increases, and exposures to systematic risks rise, compressing risk premia. Expansion into principal investment activities ensues, often without requisite organizational and risk-management capabilities. Meanwhile, difficulties of generating alpha result in many supposedly market-neutral principal investments turning to systematic risks in search for returns, which additionally compresses risk premia. Allocations to progressively more complicated financial products grow, with financial institutions and institutional investors taking on various unfamiliar risks.

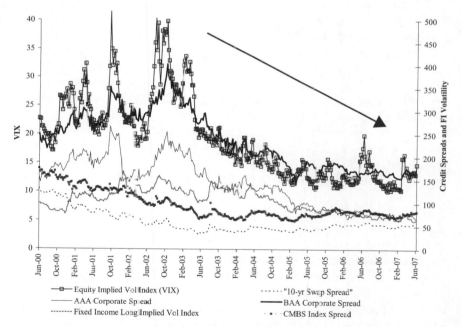

FIGURE 3.1 The Compression of Risk Premia (2003–2006)

Source: Federal Reserve, Bloomberg, Bear Stearns.

Systematic risks have always been critical to the process of economic value creation by financial institutions. However, accounting standards, financial disclosures, buy-and-hold practices, and the old ways of thinking have often obscured the evolving role of systematic risks in the generation of economic performance. When risk premia are high and a large proportion of economic performance is generated through market-insensitive balance sheet arbitrage and fees, as was often the case during the Golden Age, there is more room for error related to hidden or misunderstood risks. However, as fees and balance sheet arbitrage decline and risk premia compress, the importance of dynamic risk taking increases, and the cyclicality and volatility of static business models becomes readily apparent. In this regard, a provocative ongoing debate revolves around the question of whether as a result of various secular forces, risk premia have *on average* experienced a secular compression as well, as suggested by the persistent declines in both bank and insurance net interest margins over the past 10 years. In fact, while a portion of the margin compression in the banking industry can be explained by the compression of the balance sheet arbitrage component of economic performance, this argument does not hold in the case of the insurance industry. The jury on this issue is still out, especially considering the extreme rise in risk premia around the time when this book is going into publication.

If a financial institution or an institutional investor desires to deliver a meaningful portion of economic performance through dynamic management of systematic risks, a rigorous senior executive-level ("top-down") investment process must be set up. The corresponding cultural change is required as well: It must be acknowledged that taking on active views on systematic risks entails an entirely different organizational structure, executive skills, analytical tools, and decision-making processes as opposed to growth of static A/L businesses or diversification of principal investments. Dynamic management of systematic risks is bound to play an increasingly important role in the economic performance of financial institutions, affecting the cyclicality of earnings, impacting equity market valuations, and serving as one of the main determinants of success and failure altogether.

Fees and Expenses $(+F - E)$

The components of economic performance corresponding to fees (F) and expenses (E) are self-explanatory: Financial institutions remain focused on growing fee-based businesses and controlling expenses. Of special relevance for business model and economic performance discussions, the importance of fee-based businesses tends to increase—with the fight for them intensifying—whenever the differential returns between assets and liabilities decline. The same applies to the focus on expense management during periods of margin compressions.

Capital Structure Optimization (C_C)

The total cost of an institution's capital structure reflects a number of different factors: (a) the institution's credit rating, (b) relative proportions of broad categories of capital securities within the capital structure, and (c) sizes, structures, and maturities of instruments within each category. Capital structure optimization (C_C), which is often referred to as the *minimization of the weighted average after-tax cost of capital*, has become an increasingly important component of economic value creation in recent years as financial institutions have been afforded increased flexibility with respect to debt funding and capital raising alternatives. For the purposes of this book and consistent with investment banking conventions, we will use the terms *minimization of the cost of capital* and *capital structure optimization* interchangeably, subject to the acknowledgment that the latter is a broader task of not only minimizing the cost of capital but also balancing a plethora of regulatory, rating agency, and capital market considerations. Recall that in the derivation of the risk-based economic performance equation, I assumed that the total cost of the firm's capital was represented by the cost of its shareholders' equity. Of course, the modern view of the firm's capital structure additionally involves senior and subordinated debt instruments, debt-like hybrid capital securities, convertible bonds, and preferred stocks. The existence of the debt/equity continuum implies that there are alternative ways in which the line between liabilities and equity of a company can be drawn, which poses organizational and conceptual implications. In fact, capital structure optimization exercises may affect other components of the economic performance equation, particularly systematic risks. For instance, if a credit rating of an institution changes as a result of a deliberate capital-related or business decision, asset/liability factor loadings are likely to be affected as wholesale liabilities are remapped onto a different set of systematic risk factors. This suggests that systematic risk management and capital management should be a part of an integrated enterprise-wide process. The task of capital structure optimization should continue to evolve as the financial industry continues to move toward *risk-focused* regulation and risk-management-based executive decision making.

Economic Performance Attribution

The risk-based economic performance equation provides important insights into the process of economic value creation by modern financial institutions. Additionally, it helps describe the risk/return characteristics of different business model mixes: For example, the risk inherent in an institution that generates the vast majority of economic performance through balance sheet arbitrage should be substantially less than that of a firm that creates the majority of economic value through principal investment activities.

Let us define the proportions of economic performance due to individual risk-based components as *economic performance attribution ratios*. As it is often the case with financial heuristics, economic performance attribution ratios can be defined in various ways depending on what decision makers find intuitive and useful. Using balance sheet arbitrage as an example, I define economic performance attribution corresponding to a particular component of risk-based economic performance as follows:

$$EPA_{ARB} = \frac{\alpha_{ARB}}{\alpha_{ARB} + \alpha_{PI} + \sum \beta_i \cdot RP_i + F - E}$$

Other components' economic performance attribution ratios can be defined analogously. Corresponding numerical illustrations can be found in Appendix B.

The language of economic performance attribution enables concise descriptions of business models, leading to the following observations about real-world financial institutions:

- Business models of the portfolio businesses of housing *government-sponsored enterprises* (GSE) in the United States entail raising funds at submarket levels due to implicit government guarantees, investing proceeds in mortgage-backed securities and loans, and hedging out the majority of differential interest-rate risks. Economic performance, therefore, can be attributed to the following two dominant components: balance sheet arbitrage (e.g., negative agency/LIBOR basis) and compensation for taking on systematic risk factors (e.g., mortgage/LIBOR option-adjusted spread).[5] For those GSEs that have both portfolio and credit-guarantee businesses, economic performance is comprised of balance sheet arbitrage, systematic risks, and fees. Importantly, in this setting, short options embedded in the credit-guarantee business belong to the systematic risk component of economic performance rather than the fee component. Proportions of economic performance due to various risk-based components—the portfolio of risk-based business models—can be described through the attribution ratios that may vary over time.
- Liabilities of *commercial banks* are becoming more sensitive to changes in interest rates, which is diminishing the balance sheet arbitrage component of economic performance. To combat margin pressures, depositories are growing fee-based businesses and increasingly relying on principal investments and systematic risks to create economic value. Economic performance attribution can help compare the old versus the

new composition of economic performance during this evolutionary transformation from static to dynamic business models. Meanwhile, the lack of risk-based transparency about the process may affect equity market valuations, as shown in Appendix B, which calls for proactive stakeholder communication.

- Responding to a tougher competitive landscape and fee compression, *securities firms* are embarking on business model transformations where strategic advisory businesses are integrated with principal investment and financing activities. In the process, as can be shown through economic performance attribution, business models with a high proportion of economic performance coming from fees are giving way to business models where principal investments and systematic risks are playing much greater roles. Among other things, this appears to be contributing to the compression of price-to-earnings ratios of securities firms relative to historical norms.

The risk-based economic performance equation represents all earnings drivers in a consistent fashion that is grounded in economic reality. It helps filter out the complexity of the modern world of finance and connect the seemingly disparate macroeconomic and financial phenomena. Importantly, it formally separates risk taking from other economic value-generating activities, such as fees and balance sheet arbitrage, thus defining the role of risk management in executive decision making.

In turn, economic performance attribution affords a straightforward description of financial institutions' business models, with the respective roles of fee-based and risk-taking activities clearly delineated. As illustrated in Appendix B, economic performance attribution goes hand-in-hand with modern risk-management tools in articulating risk/return characteristics of business models and providing a framework for optimization of risk-adjusted economic performance. As financial institutions move toward risk-based disclosures and fair valuation, economic performance attribution should become more directly linked to equity market valuations, which I discuss in detail in Chapter 5. Last, economic performance attribution ratios have relevance for risk-focused regulation since similarly chartered institutions may exhibit drastically different risk-based business models and overall risk exposures.

Having explained the drivers of economic performance through the risk-based economic performance equation, I turn next to describing the choices, tools, and practical solutions available to senior decision makers endeavoring to respond to the evolutionary challenges of the dynamic new world.

CHAPTER 4

Business Model Transformations

Pillars of Strategic Decisions in a Dynamic World

The last two chapters of this book are devoted to the detailed discussion of *Financial Darwinism*—a practical and actionable decision-making framework designed to give financial executives the tools necessary to navigate the ongoing tectonic financial shift. I begin this chapter with a discussion of the four pillars of strategic decisions in the dynamic new world—business strategy combined with corporate finance, accounting earnings, risk management, and investment analysis—and their role in the desired evolutionary responses to the challenges faced by traditional financial businesses.

So far in this book, we have spent a fair amount of time looking at the old regime, where static (from the risk-taking perspective) business models produced adequate earnings in an environment of high fees and generous asset/liability spreads. In that setting, financial executives were focused on creating robust business mixes, growing individual businesses through a variety of business- and customer-related activities, generating stable and growing accounting earnings, controlling expenses, preserving strategic flexibility, and striving for premium equity market valuation of their firms.

In the dynamic new world, however, as static business models come under pressures and active risk taking starts to play a more prominent role in economic value creation, accounting earnings and business strategy cannot remain the sole inputs to strategic decisions. Other pillars—namely, risk management and investment analyses—get an equally visible seat at the table where strategic decisions are being made. In Figure 4.1, Investment Analysis is a catchall for a vast array of approaches to making investment decisions. Of particular importance to this book are investment analyses that allow the formulation of views on various systematic risk factors, such as interest rates, yield curves, mortgage prepayments, credit spreads and defaults, implied volatilities, equities, commodities, and currencies. These views are usually based on both fundamental (related to

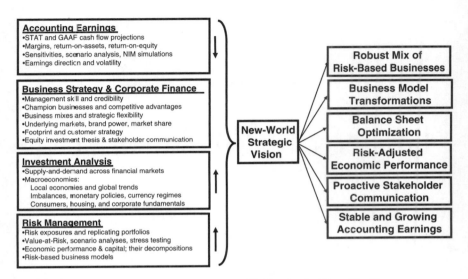

FIGURE 4.1 Four Pillars of Strategic Decision Making in the New World

macroeconomics) and technical (related to supply-and-demand) considerations. As for the Risk Management pillar in Figure 4.1, it brings the entire arsenal of modern risk-measurement and risk-management techniques and approaches into the realm of executive decisions. This pillar encompasses risk-based business models that underlie the risk-based economic performance equation as well as such modern risk measures as Value-at-Risk, economic capital, partial durations, scenario analyses, and stress tests (see Appendix B).

The task of managing financial institutions has always been a combination of art and science that relied on the executives' ability to constantly marry a plethora of business decisions, rigorous financial analyses, subjective judgments, capital market and regulatory considerations, and various real-life constraints. This book argues that the job of a financial executive has become progressively harder over recent decades, as business and macroeconomic environments became more complex and uncertain and the pressures facing the providers of basic (and increasingly commoditized) financial services intensified. As with other settings where Darwinian organisms strive to survive and succeed in the game of natural selection, the ability and willingness of modern financial institutions to adapt to the dynamic new world is paramount. What does this entail? First, the transition from the old regime to the dynamic new world is accompanied by the significant evolution of the executive decision-making process, expanding decision-making pillars and changing their relative importance over time. Second, the change in the nature of economic value creation necessitates a broader perspective and an expanded skill set on the part of financial executives and their strategic advisors. Third, the process of adaptation is ongoing: Even when an organization has successfully transformed itself, it cannot stand still but must continue to reassess and rebalance its resources, businesses, and risks as business and market environments change around it.

Let us now examine in detail how the introduction of two new pillars of strategic decision making—a reflection of the changed task of economic value creation in the dynamic world—affects the nature of strategic vision, management decisions, the notion of optimality, and the essence of stakeholder communication. While as before our focus will remain on financial institutions, many of the ideas presented are relevant to financial activities of non-financial corporations as well.

Responsive Recalibrations of Business Models

As modern financial institutions and institutional investors are adapting to the new order, executive decisions directed at more proactive and dynamic economic value creation can be thought of as falling into the following two general categories.

- *Responsive recalibrations of business models*: Transitions from static to dynamic business models, where *individual components* of the economic performance equation are continually enhanced; and
- *Full-scale business model transformations*: Dynamic rebalancing of risk-based business model mixes on the *enterprise-wide level*. This, among other things, includes the maximization of synergies among different businesses, resulting in the whole enterprise becoming more valuable and effective than the sum of its parts.

This section deals with the former category of executive actions, describing how business strategy combined with corporate finance, risk management, and investment activities can be effectively employed in this regard. As a reminder, the risk-based economic performance equation whose individual components are to be enhanced is as follows.

$$EP = \alpha_{Arb} + \alpha_{PI} + \sum \beta_i \cdot RP_i + F - E - C_C$$

Improvement of Economic Performance: Balance Sheet Arbitrage (α_{Arb})

Balance sheet arbitrage is generated on the liability side of the balance sheet, which makes business strategy and corporate finance the appropriate means of sustaining and enhancing this component of economic performance. In terms of retail liabilities of commercial banks, the following arsenal of activities—improvements in customer service, client-retention strategies via cross-selling of products and services, marketing exercises that increase an institution's brand power—can be employed to reduce the cost of liabilities as well as their sensitivity to changes in interest rates. As for the wholesale liabilities of government-sponsored enterprises that also enjoy balance sheet arbitrage, in addition to deepening risk management sophistication, GSEs can use investment banking and marketing activities to expand the universe of their debt and capital investors worldwide and facilitate product innovation on the liability side of the balance sheet, thus maintaining and even improving their funding levels.

Improvement of Economic Performance: Principal Investments (α_{PI})

Principal investments are becoming an important feature of business models of financial institutions and institutional investors, serving as one of the more pervasive examples of the ongoing movement away from static business models. To introduce this component of economic performance into the business mix and continually enhance it over time, the desired role of principal investments in the overall business model needs to be crystallized, which has a number of conceptual and organizational aspects. First, the overall risk budget corresponding to principal investments must be determined and institutionalized. Second, in some sense *optimal* portfolio of principal investments—consisting of capital allocations to proprietary desks, hedge funds and private equity funds under management, and venture capital, hedge fund, or private equity investments made directly by the institution—must be created. Third, a rigorous risk-management process must be put in place on the enterprise-wide, business segment, and individual investment levels, with adequate risk limits and concentration analyses ensuring proper diversification. Forth, in order to ensure that this type of active risk taking does not lead to unpleasant surprises, executives and risk managers must continuously monitor the nature of risks embedded in this by-construction market-neutral component of economic performance, making sure that it does not have any hidden structural systematic risks. Finally, investment and risk-management personnel must be chosen to collectively have the adequate expertise and command of advanced financial instruments, products, investment strategies, and tools. Further details on the matter can be found in the Executive Action Plan for implementing the framework proposed in this book (Chapter 5).

Improvement of Economic Performance: Systematic Risks $(\sum \beta_i \cdot P_i)$

Dynamic management of systematic risks on the enterprise-wide level is increasingly used by financial institutions and institutional investors to transition away from static business models and explore new ways of creating economic value. Progressively more active management of foreign exchange risks, interest-rate risks, and pension plan A/L exposures represents the analogous trend involving non-financial corporations.

When it comes to this component of economic performance, financial executives and their strategic advisors typically use such organizational structures as asset/liability committees (ALCOs) to implement the top-down firm-wide risk-taking process of dynamically rebalancing systematic risks. As with principal investments, determining the overall risk budget corresponding to this type of risk-taking comes first. The difference relative to principal investments, of course, lies in the next step: As opposed to making one-off investments or selecting traders and external asset managers who would subsequently make their own investment decisions subject to risk limits, here a portfolio of desired systematic risks is created and continuously managed on the enterprise-wide level.

As an illustration, consider a hypothetical top-down ALCO process directed at generating economic performance through a dynamic rebalancing of systematic risks over long horizons. It can start, for instance, with economists and market strategists formulating expectations of systematic risk factors' behavior as a function of various stages of an economic cycle, as shown in Table 4.1. In the process, fundamental views must be married with supply-and-demand-related considerations.

Subsequently, systematic risks on the balance sheet or portfolio level can be dynamically rebalanced in accordance with these economic and market views. In anticipation of a slowdown or recession, for instance, differential asset/liability exposures may be positioned to benefit from a decline in interest rates, a steepening of the yield curve, deterioration of credit fundamentals, and an increase in mortgage prepayments. On the contrary, a transition into an economic expansion may warrant pairing down interest-rate risk; exiting "borrow short/lend long" carry trades, increasing exposures to equities, credit, and emerging markets; and positioning for a slowdown in mortgage prepayments. The latter scenario is described in Figure 4.2, which also lists major systematic risks, corresponding risk measures, and hedging instruments typically used to readjust these exposures. Notice the important new source of flexibility in economic value creation emphasized in this

TABLE 4.1   Hypothetical Market Expectations for Different Stages
of an Economic Cycle

Monetary Policy & Systematic Risks	Stages of Economic Cycle	
	Slowdown & Recession	Recovery & Expansion
Monetary Policy	Easier/Accommodative	Tighter/Restrictive
Interest Rates	Decline	Rise
Yield Curves	Steepen	Flatten
Credit Spreads	Widen	Tighten
Credit Defaults	Rise	Decline
Mortgage Prepayments	Speed up	Slow down
Equities	Sell off	Rally

figure: Systematic risks can be dynamically rebalanced within an evolving
risk budget to reflect changing market views. This presents a stark contrast
to the typical behavior of institutions with static business models, where the
transition into an adverse environment is usually accompanied by lower risk
tolerance and deleveraging—precisely because underlying systematic risks
are not explicitly managed. Obviously, such behavior may lead to cyclical
earnings profiles and high opportunity costs.

Note that while the previous example deals with balance sheet management where systematic risk taking involves differential risk exposures
between assets and liabilities, the same investment process can apply to
managing investment portfolios, both in absolute terms and relative to
benchmarks.

Risk Type	Risk Measure	Typical Hedges
Interest Rate Level	Duration, convexity, principal components, scenario analysis, stress testing, Value-at-Risk	Treasuries, agencies, interest rate derivatives, Treasury and eurodollar futures, OTC options
Yield Cyrve Shape	Key rate durations, principal components, scenario analysis, stress testing, Value-at-Risk	Same as above as well as structured notes
Prepayment	Mortgage basis and prepayment durations, PORC	IOs, POs, CMOs, Alt-A and other mortgage "story" bonds
Volatility	Volatility durations, Value-at-Risk	Swaptions, caps, floors, OTC options, callable and puttable securities, mortgages, CMOs
Credit Spread (as market risk)	Spread duration, Value-at-Risk, holdings limits (by credit rating)	Interest rate swaps, agencies, credit default swaps
Equity	Betas, Value-at-Risk, stress testing	Equity derivatives, asset allocation
Commodity	Notional exposures, Value-at-Risk greeks, stress testing	Commodity futures and options

FIGURE 4.2   Hypothetical Rebalancing of Systematic Risks In Anticiaption of an
Economic Recovery

As is the case with principal investments, the desire to deliver consistent and growing economic performance through dynamic management of systematic risks presents new opportunities as well as numerous new challenges. First, the expansion of the investment universe on the part of financial institutions and institutional investors is particularly noteworthy in this regard: New types of investments and new systematic risks, such as commodities, currencies, local-currency emerging markets, are continuously added to the investment arsenal in order to increase strategic flexibility and improve expected risk-adjusted performance. Second, dynamic risk-taking decisions along the lines of Figure 4.2 represent a dramatic departure from the skill sets, organizational structures, and tools employed by executives in financial institutions with static business models. A rigorous top-down asset-liability management process, sophisticated risk-management capabilities, and command of advanced financial tools that can be used to implement investment views become paramount. Third, understanding the dynamics of modern financial crises—and recognizing asset bubbles in the making—becomes an important aspect of the dynamic management of systematic risks. The nature and content of stakeholder communication by companies who embark on improving this component of economic performance must change accordingly: The executives' strategic vision as well as their track record of active risk taking become important ingredients of economic value creation in this setting and need to be articulated as such in order to achieve premium equity valuation.

Improvement of Economic Performance: Fees and Expenses $(+ F - E)$

A variety of activities that typically fall under the umbrella of business strategy combined with corporate finance can be proactively used by modern financial institutions to grow fee-based businesses and control expenses. Of particular importance to this component of economic performance is the advent of *securitization*—the process of pooling together assets and receivables, repackaging them as financial instruments, and selling them to investors. Securitization has become an important new source of fee income that, if properly risk managed, can transform risk-taking businesses (such as loan origination) into fee-based businesses. In an equally significant development, asset management has become an integral part of business mixes of financial institutions and an important fee-based revenue source. Given dominant demographic and macroeconomic factors (just think of pensions and sovereign wealth funds), asset-gathering strategies and asset-management product innovation should remain the focus of the firms who desire to improve this component of the economic performance equation. Notice that while gathering of assets under management typically falls under business strategy, creation of economic value *within* asset-management products rests on the other pillars of strategic decision making: investment analysis and risk management.

As for expenses, financial institutions continue to be proactive and innovative in minimizing expenses through mergers and acquisitions, technological innovation, applications of the management science, and other business strategy and corporate finance activities. A fuller elaboration of specific expense-minimization strategies employed by financial institutions is beyond the scope of this book.

Improvement of Economic Performance: Capital Structure Optimization (C_C)

Minimization of the total cost of the firm's capital structure has become an important component of economic performance in recent years. Typically, investment banks and other strategic advisors are retained by financial institutions and non-financial companies to analyze the alternatives and subsequently underwrite and sell debt and capital instruments to investors worldwide. Today, when a plethora of funding and capital choices exists—ranging from common and preferred stocks to various forms of debt instruments and hybrid capital securities—capital structure optimization has become a nontrivial act of balancing capital market perceptions, taxes, regulatory requirements, and credit-rating considerations as well as exploiting the so-called "regulatory and credit rating arbitrage." The objective of maintaining and enhancing the firm's flexibility to make important strategic investments and organically grow various businesses remains an important dimension of capital management. In certain cases, hybrid capital issuance is coupled with the use of sophisticated financial technology that allows financial institutions and corporations to buy back their own stock in accounting- and tax-efficient ways, which can reduce the total cost of capital and potentially improve equity valuations. As emphasized before, capital structure optimization exercises may simultaneously affect other components of the economic performance equation (namely, systematic risks), which suggests that responsive recalibrations of business models that involve capital management should be a part of an integrated enterprise-wide process.

Full-Scale Business Model Transformations

Financial Darwinism encompasses a plethora of executive decisions that help financial institutions adapt to the new reality and enhance economic performance in a dynamic fashion. In particular, there are two distinct categories of such decisions. The first one, covered in the previous section, is comprised of responsive recalibrations of business models—transitions from static to dynamic business models where individual components of the economic performance equation are enhanced. The second entails full-scale business model transformations, where entire portfolios of risk-based business models are dynamically and continuously rebalanced over time. This section deals with the latter category and illustrates various choices and dilemmas that accompany comprehensive business model transformations.

To illustrate the decision-making process surrounding the myriad alternatives facing today's financial executives, consider the following nontrivial choices and dilemmas: Do I grow risk-taking businesses or fee-based businesses? Among risk-taking businesses, do I emphasize asset/liability spread businesses (e.g., commercial lending) versus principal investments? Where and how do I use short options to increase my returns? Among fee-based businesses, do I prefer brokerage to strategic advisory or asset management? What is my view on the use of "originate-securitize-and-sell" business models in commercial banking or insurance businesses?

The universe of critical business model-related choices facing financial executives is shown in Figure 4.3. First and foremost, assuming that balance sheet arbitrage, expenses, and capital structure have already been individually optimized through various business strategy and corporate finance activities (responsive recalibrations), the following fundamental decision needs to be made: *What is the desired proportion of economic performance that is generated through risk-taking activities vis-à-vis fee-based activities?* This decision—based on the institution's (a) business legacy; (b) strategic vision of executives; (c) unique circumstances, objectives, and constrains; and (d) external environment—reflects the value proposition of the institution, its risk-taking philosophy, as well as its overall risk tolerance (*risk budget*), dramatically affecting all subsequent decisions.

Figure 4.3 shows that once the role of risk-taking activities vis-à-vis fee-based businesses—and their relative desirability—has been determined, more specific choices of risk-based and fee-based businesses within each category should be analyzed. Within the systematic risk component, the investment universe of asset classes or, equivalently, risk dimensions needs to be established, with the desired role of short options in the generation of economic performance clearly identified. Subsequently, responsive recalibrations of business models that dynamically manage systematic risks can be performed. Among principal investment activities, the roles of various types of activities—proprietary trading, hedge funds and private equity funds under management, and direct private equity and venture capital investments—can be periodically reassessed, again in the spirit of responsive recalibrations. The same applies to various dimensions of fee-based businesses. As mentioned before, this book uses the simplest possible

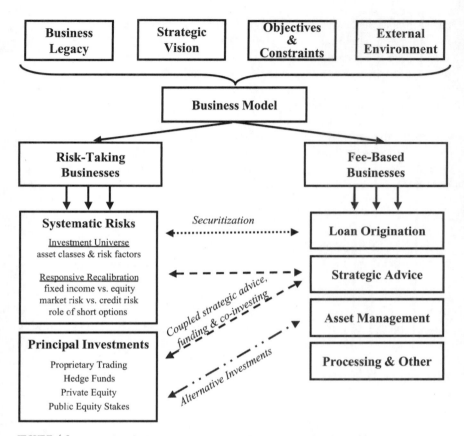

FIGURE 4.3 Example of a Dynamic Strategic Management Decision Tree

classification of risk-based business models—conceptually distinct risk-taking and fee-generating activities—to explain risk-based economic performance and identify the choices facing modern executives. The same decision-making process can be also extended to more elaborate taxonomies of risk-based business models.[1]

Once the individual business decisions and preferences in Figure 4.3 have been distilled, the art of marrying business strategy, corporate finance, risk-based business models, and investment decisions begins. At this stage, executives must answer yet another important set of questions: Should strategic advisory services be coupled with principal investment and financing activities, as shown via lines connecting Strategic Advice, Principle Investments, and Systematic Risks in Figure 4.3; and if so, how should potential conflicts of interest be anticipated? Should growth of asset-management fee businesses be intertwined with principal investments, for instance, through hedge funds under management? Should originated loans be retained on the balance sheet as is, or hedged, or securitized and sold (with the latter choice effectively converting a risk-taking business model into a fee-based business model)? Should reinsurance be used to eliminate out-of-the-money short options on the balance sheet? Notice that the language of risk-based business naturally lends itself onto such a discussion since it operates in terms of conceptually different risk-taking or fee-based activities; making similar choices in terms of asset classes or business segment classifications typically used in financial disclosures would be much more cumbersome. The outcome of a decision-making process presented in Figure 4.3 is the desired mix of risk-based business models that reflects strategic vision of executives as well as numerous objectives, considerations, and constraints unique to the institution. In the spirit of dynamism, it must be performed on a regular basis.

The term *full-scale business model transformations* is reflective of the fact that the decision-making process shown in Figure 4.3 can yield different business model mixes over time as the strategic vision of executives and their risk tolerances evolve as a function of new realities, environments, and opportunities. This leads to an interesting comparison: Business model mixes of financial institutions can be thought of as analogous to strategic asset allocations of institutional investors. The difference, of course, lies in institutional investors making allocations to asset classes, whereas financial institutions make capital (or risk-budget) allocations to risk-based business models. As empirical studies have shown, strategic asset allocations (or "policies") determine the overwhelming majority of both returns and risks of institutional investors.[2] By extension, this book argues that full-scale business model transformations are by far the most influential type of executive decisions in the dynamic new world, which naturally makes strategic vision one of the critical determinants of value creation and success. Once full-scale business model transformations yield desired business mixes, responsive recalibrations of business models and optimizations of absolute and risk-adjusted economic performance can be employed to further refine and formalize various choices, serving as analogs of tactical asset allocations, manager selection, and various other forms of alpha generation by institutional investors—activities that are all important yet secondary in terms of their impacts on the overall performance.

In order to further illustrate these points, let us examine some of the decisions related to business model transformations by different kinds of financial institutions.

Decisions by Commercial Banks

Commercial banks are already moving away from static business models whose profitability is largely determined by differential returns between

unmanaged and held-to-maturity assets and liabilities. In an attempt to reduce the cyclicality of their earnings and alter risk/return profiles, commercial banks have undertaken a variety of activities that improve individual
components of economic performance as well as transform business models over time. In one of the most obvious examples, securitization has been
routinely used to transform risk-taking loan origination businesses into fee-
generating businesses—the practice that has played an important role in
the winding up as well as unwinding of some of the notable market crises
of the past decade. In other examples of dynamic behavior, concentrated
risk exposures are now routinely mitigated through cash securitizations as
well as synthetic securitizations, credit derivatives, total return swaps, and a
variety of other advanced products and strategies.

Dynamic management of systematic risks has also become an increasingly important source of economic value creation by commercial banks.

- When C & I loan demand declines and/or as credit fundamentals dete-
  riorate during recessions, banks often increase their holdings of mortgages and other high-credit-quality fixed-income securities, thus substituting credit risk with market risk on their balance sheets over time, as
  shown in Figure 4.4. Conversely, as C & I loan demand comes back
  and credit fundamentals improve, exposures may be reversed. Thus,
  in the spirit of the previous section and Figure 4.2, the systematic risk
  component of economic performance is enhanced through dynamic

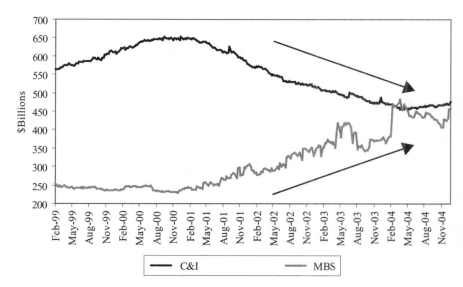

FIGURE 4.4 C&I and MBS Holdings of U.S. Commercial Banks

management, within a constant or evolving risk budgets, depending on the circumstances. As I have mentioned earlier, this presents a stark contrast to the *modus operandi* associated with static business models where instead of rebalancing of risks, the size of the balance sheet is adjusted to reflect the view on the environment while the underlying risks remain the same.

- During the periods of monetary easing, banks may amplify borrow short/lend long carry trades, making their balance sheets *liability-sensitive*. Yield curve exposures are often reversed, with durations of assets and liabilities matched closer, as the environment shifts toward the monetary tightening and a potential yield curve inversion.

Last, large commercial banks in the United States combated compressing net interest margins by growing fee-based businesses, as shown in Figure 4.5. This included income from fiduciary activities, service charges on deposit accounts, trading revenues, fees and commissions from securities brokerage, investment banking advisory and underwriting fees, fees and commissions from annuity sales, underwriting income from insurance and reinsurance activities, servicing fees, and securitization income. Along with better expense management, the increase in the relative proportion of revenues due to noninterest income allowed commercial banks to maintain

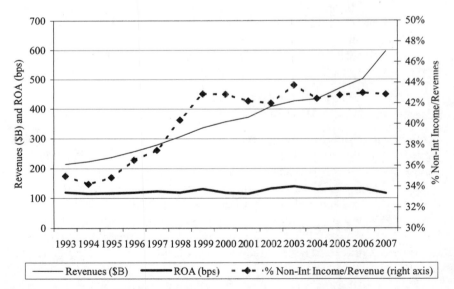

FIGURE 4.5 Revenues, ROA, and Non-Interest Income of U.S. Commercial Banks
Sources: FDIC.

stable levels of returns-on-assets (ROAs) despite the margin compression shown in Table 2.2.

Decisions on Writing Options

The role of short options in the generation of economic performance represents one of the most intriguing examples of how different risk-taking philosophies affect business models of financial institutions. Consider the following two alternative balance sheet strategies, both designed to increase the differential returns between assets and liabilities through short options:

1. Write at-the-money options by increasing allocations to callable bonds, mortgage-backed securities, collateralized mortgage obligations, and certain structured notes. Spend a portion of the resulting excess return on buying out-of-the-money option-based protection against catastrophic events, thus reducing tail risk.
2. Write out-of-the money options via range-accrual structured notes, caps, floors, or other derivatives embedded in either assets or liabilities. Alternatively, purchase a reinsurance company.

Both actions—employed by real-world commercial banks, securities firms, hedge funds, and other financial institutions—are indicative of conceptually different approaches to delivering economic performance via systematic risk exposures. Note that neither of these approaches is intrinsically superior in general terms: They simply represent alternative strategic visions on the role of short options in the "optimal" risk-based business model mixes.

Decisions on Business Mixes Involving Mortgage Servicing Companies

Dilemmas regarding the role of mortgage servicing companies in business mixes of commercial banks and other financial institutions illustrate the nontrivial interaction of risk-based business models, investment analyses, business strategy, and corporate finance. As a matter of background, assets of mortgage servicing companies mainly consist of mortgage servicing rights (MSRs) that generally resemble interest-only, stripped mortgage-backed securities.[3] MSRs are characterized by very large risk exposures to interest rates and mortgage prepayments and, therefore, can generate significant volatility of accounting earnings as well as economic performance.

Following the general train of thought depicted in Figure 4.3, strategic discussions by executive management regarding MSRs often begin with the following question: "What is the precise rationale of having a mortgage servicing company as part of the business mix of an institution?" Two contrasting potential responses to this question are as follows.

1. The mortgage servicing company represents a gateway to consumers that improves the institution's balance sheet arbitrage (e.g., via cross-selling) as well as credit characteristics of its mortgage loan holdings. Without these attributes, mortgage servicing rights would not be viewed as an appealing holding on the balance sheet.
2. Risk/return characteristics of mortgage servicing rights—taken in the context of an institution's balance sheet—make MSRs a desirable asset class in its own right. Additionally, MSRs may fulfill other secondary business and risk-management roles.

Notice an important distinction between the two viewpoints. In the first one, MSRs represent not a risk-taking but rather a business decision. Therefore, risk exposures should be completely hedged out, which would result in a business model recalibration. In the second case, the mortgage servicing company is a deliberate investment or risk-taking decision, with corporate finance being a secondary consideration. In that case, MSRs should be included as a part of an integrated balance sheet management process, both in terms of security-specific risks (principal investment component of economic performance) as well as systematic risks.

Making the Strategic Vision a Reality

The Arsenal of Advanced Financial Tools for Strategic Decisions

A consistent theme of this book is that success and even survival of modern financial institutions depend on the executives' strategic vision of what constitutes an *optimal* mix of risk-based business models. In this regard, as contrasted in Figure 2.1 versus Figure 4.1, the transition from the old regime to the dynamic new world is accompanied by the expansion of the pillars of decision making and the change of the nature of strategic vision. Meanwhile, proactive risk-taking decisions and business model transformations become progressively more important to the process of economic value creation, largely determining successes and failures.

Not surprisingly, the overall effectiveness of such broad institutional endeavors greatly depends on executives' abilities to implement their visions through a combination of financial and organizational means. *The optimality of the implementation process, therefore, should go hand in hand with the* optimality *of the strategic vision itself*. This section focuses in on the conceptual issues of making strategic vision a reality. Related organizational

FIGURE 4.6 The Arsenal of Advanced Financial Tools Used in Implementing a Strategic Vision

matters are presented in summary form in the Executive Action Plan (Chapter 5).

Let us return to the decision tree in Figure 4.3, which illustrates the process of determining the desired portfolio of risk-based business models on the enterprise-wide level. Each arrow in this diagram represents a critical executive decision that is based on a plethora of external as well as unique-to-the-institution considerations and is in need of decision support. Additionally, each decision (path on the decision tree) lends itself onto a number of possible implementation strategies.

The arsenal of advanced financial tools that can be used by modern financial executives to implement their strategic vision is presented in Figure 4.6. It includes mergers and acquisitions (M & A), asset strategies, debt management, securitization, derivatives hedging, product design, insurance, leverage, and changes in the capital structure. Not surprisingly, these tools go hand-in-hand with business model transformations and pillars of strategic decisions discussed throughout this chapter, affording executives both the decision-making framework to formulate a strategic vision as well as significant flexibility with respect to its implementation.

In this day and age, capital market innovations afford us with a variety of alternative solutions for any particular problem. For instance, recall the discussion surrounding systematic risk management depicted in Figure 4.2. In that example, a hypothetical financial institution decided to pair down the interest-rate risk on its balance sheet in anticipation of an economic expansion, tighter monetary policy, and rising interest rates. Once the strategic decision regarding systematic risks has been made on the top executive level, the best implementation strategy needs to be determined using the entire universe of financial and business tools. Thus, the reduction of a balance sheet's interest-rate risk can be equivalently achieved through (a) debt restructuring, (b) asset rebalancing, (c) derivatives hedging, (d) securitization, or (e) purchasing a mortgage servicing company. The necessary change in the executive skill set referred to repeatedly in this book thus becomes self-evident: Decision makers must collectively gain an intimate familiarity with the entire arsenal of advanced financial tools in order to implement the strategic vision in an optimal way and maximize economic performance.

Optimization of Risk-Adjusted Economic Performance

Strategic vision, advanced financial tools, decision support systems, and subjective judgment are the facets of implicit conceptual optimization problems underlying the management of modern financial institutions. However, as financial executives and their strategic advisors would attest, explicitly using computer optimization systems to formulate executive-level strategic vision and arrive at a desired mix of risk-based business models is very difficult in practice. There are simply too many subjective elements, unique institutional circumstances and constraints, and other external factors that serve as inputs into such high-level decisions. This is why I illustrated this process via the decision tree shown in Figure 4.3. However, once important philosophical choices have been made on the enterprise-wide level, the implementation stage can involve more formal optimization exercises. While objective function and constraints of such optimizations evolve over time to reflect changing risk/return tradeoffs and capital market considerations, arriving at a robust business mix, achieving premium equity valuation, minimizing the cost of capital, and preserving strategic flexibility are likely to remain among the most important goals of financial institutions, which is consistent with the message of Figure 4.1. In this regard, making the maximization of absolute and risk-adjusted economic performance a part of the objective function can seamlessly integrate *Financial Darwinism* into the existing practices of financial institutions. Risk-based business models can be used as levers in these optimizations, and economic performance attribution ratios can go hand-in-hand with risk measures when defining objective functions, as illustrated in Appendix B. Meanwhile, risk exposures can be described through summary measures (e.g., economic capital and Value-at-Risk that capture all embedded risks and afford meaningful risk decompositions), stress tests, scenario analyses, and parametric risk measures.[4]

In a practical and realistic caveat to this book's focus on economic performance and risk-based paradigm, the delivery of stable and growing accounting earnings remains the governing reality and the overriding objective of financial institutions as this book is written. While economic value creation is often acknowledged as the determinant of long-term viability, the dominant lens used by regulators, rating agencies, equity analysts, and various stakeholders to understand financial intermediaries and determine their equity valuations remains that of accounting earnings. Therefore, a potential solution for financial institutions in transition from the old regime to the dynamic new world involves a simultaneous optimization of both accounting earnings and risk-adjusted economic performance coupled with proactive stakeholder education. While conflicts and competing objectives may arise as economic and accounting realities are merged, such dual accounting earnings and economic performance optimizations could become a natural first step in the movement toward full-fledged dynamic management of financial institutions. Alternatively, the optimization problem can be defined as the maximization of absolute or risk-adjusted economic performance subject to various risk and accounting earnings constraints.

Although this may sound like heresy at a time when accounting earnings remain the dominant measure of a firm's performance, I believe that the balance of power in strategic decisions is likely to gradually shift away from accounting earnings and toward economic performance. I predicate this expectation on the continuing movement toward fair valuation, risk-based financial disclosures, and risk-focused regulation. In a world focused on risk-adjusted economic performance as opposed to accounting earnings, the language of credit ratings, equity market analyses, and regulatory disclosures would likely evolve in a similar direction. In such a setting, modern risk measures are likely to replace credit ratings and earnings volatilities as representations of inherent risks, whereas drivers of earnings are likely to become increasingly described in terms of risk-based business models.

The speed and frequency of business model transformations are likely to intensify in the future, while the increasing reliance on active risk-taking decisions and skills of executives is likely to result in seemingly similar financial firms producing remarkably different financial results. As an important supplement to business model recalibrations and transformations, advanced financial tools and optimizations of risk-adjusted economic performance can be effectively used to implement the strategic vision of financial executives and sort through myriads of alternatives. The very description of the decision-making process that creates a portfolio of strategically flexible risk-based business models with desirable risk/return characteristics and enjoys a favorable view of external stakeholders suggests a need for an integrated, holistic, rigorous, and risk-focused framework.[5] Increasingly complex, uncertain, and rapidly changing market environments and competitive landscapes—full of "black swans" and "strategy paradoxes"[6]—only amplify this point and the sense of urgency.

Complexity and Decision Support

Managing modern financial institutions is a task of enormous uncertainty, scope, and complexity. This book endeavors to equip financial executives both with a coherent explanation of the evolutionary changes in the financial world as well as an actionable decision-making framework that could help formulate responses to today's challenges. By using the risk-based economic performance equation as a conceptual anchor, *Dynamic Finance* and *Financial Darwinism* go hand-in-hand in order to:

- *Filter out complexity.* Present the process of economic value creation in terms of conceptually different building blocks—the components of the risk-based economic performance equation. Financial executives are thus given a menu of broad choices on how to create or enhance economic value.
- *Help define the strategic vision* that properly delineates customer-related and risk-taking decisions. In this setting, executive-level strategic vision becomes a critical component of economic value creation, shaping the optimal mixes of risk-based business models and defining the respective roles of business strategy, corporate finance, investment analysis, and risk management.
- *Determine an* optimal *implementation strategy.* Once a decision on how to transform a business model and enhance economic performance has been made, a plethora of advanced financial tools and activities—asset strategies, liability management, securitization, M & A, derivatives hedging, and so on—can be used to implement the strategic vision in an optimal fashion.

The outcome, in the words of Oxford philosopher and friend Dr. James Wilk, is the "rich and infinitely multidimensional realm in which we can navigate our way at will amongst endless possibilities, revealing and negotiating hidden constraints, and transforming states-of-affairs all at once."[7]

So far in this book I have described the ways of adapting to the dynamic new world in relatively conceptual terms. Now it is time to look at how leading real-world financial institutions and institutional investors are already reacting to the need to change. Do they act in the spirit of *Financial Darwinism?* Are the concepts discussed in this book applicable to non-financial firms? What are the lessons learned from modern financial crises, both in terms of failures to anticipate change but also failures to manage change? Is there a need for greater transparency and, if so, what kind of transparency? These are the topics of this book's final chapter.

CHAPTER 5

The Road to Financial Darwinism

Real-World Business Model Transformations

It is fair to say that those of us who have struggled to understand the dynamic new world of finance are in good company. In fact, challenges faced by financial institutions and investors are universal in nature, brought about by a set of powerful global forces. Now, some years later, we seem to be on a path to a deeper collective understanding of the ongoing tectonic shift, having accumulated a wealth of knowledge, practical experience, and lessons learned from major market dislocations. On the pages that follow, I describe how real-world financial institutions and investors are already responding to the modern-day challenges and, importantly, how their actions relate to *Financial Darwinism*. In the process, I also use the evolutionary perspective afforded by *Dynamic Finance* to examine modern financial crises and illustrate how the changed world works in periods of distress.

We start by revisiting the descriptions of the changed financial landscape from Chapter 1, interpreting them from the viewpoint of *Dynamic Finance*, and articulating how investors and financial institutions can respond to the challenges they face in the spirit of *Financial Darwinism*.

1. "Traditional asset-allocation strategies are having trouble in today's world."

   Dynamic Finance Interpretation: Institutions that rely on static business models (or static asset allocations) are likely to deliver returns that are both cyclical and lower than historic norms.

   Financial Darwinism Response: Institutions should expand their investment universe, increase allocations to principal investments, and dynamically manage systematic risks in order to enhance economic performance.

$$\textit{Dynamic Finance Notation: } r_A - r_L \rightarrow \alpha_{PI} + \overset{\Rightarrow}{\underset{\Leftarrow}{\sum}} \beta_i P_i$$

By borrowing the notations from both the old and the new versions of the economic performance equation, the transition from a static to a dynamic business model is advocated, as illustrated in the previous formula. To emphasize that systematic risks must be continuously re-calibrated over time, the arrows around the summation sign are used.

2. "Being a great M & A advisor alone doesn't cut it anymore. Unless you can also provide a client with a multibillion-dollar financing package, you're irrelevant.

    Dynamic Finance Interpretation: Underwriting fees, commissions, and bid/ask spreads have declined while competition has increased, putting pressures on the fee-based businesses of investment banks.

    Financial Darwinism Response: Consider this CEO's quote in con-junction with his firm's view on what makes a modern investment bank effective in fulfilling the clients' needs—being an "advisor, financier, and coinvestor" all in one.[1] Thus, the proposed solution to the ongoing competitive and market pressures entails a business model transforma-tion that integrates strategic advice, financing, and principal investment activities along the lines of Figure 4.3.

$$\textit{Dynamic Finance Notation: } F \rightarrow \alpha_{PI} + \overset{\Rightarrow}{\underset{\Leftarrow}{\sum}} \beta_i P_i + F$$

    In the language of risk-based business models, a fee-based advisory business is thus transformed into a portfolio of principal investments, systematic risks, and fee-based business models, as shown in the pre-vious formula.

3. "If you want to stay alive in the asset-management business, you have to go into unique products and go out on the risk spectrum."

    Dynamic Finance Interpretation: The commoditization of core asset-management products—coupled with greater market efficiency and attendant challenges of alpha generation—translates into a very tough competitive environment.

    Financial Darwinism Response: Asset managers need to constantly innovate investment products to fulfill the evolving needs of their clients. Equally importantly, delivering superior performance across market cycles requires a continuous expansion of the investment uni-verse as well as the ability to dynamically manage a diversified portfolio of increasingly specific dimensions of risk.

$$\text{Dynamic Finance Notation: } + \overset{\Rightarrow}{\underset{\Leftarrow}{\sum}} \beta_i P_i$$

    The previous expression indicates that, inside the risk-based eco-nomic performance equation, new systematic risks are added to improve both strategic flexibility and risk-adjusted performance, with all systematic risks managed dynamically over time.

4. "We've had a tremendous golden age of [commercial] banking, and we are not going to continue to see that kind of performance."

   Dynamic Finance Interpretation: Depository institutions are likely to experience continuing earnings pressure due to the secular compression of balance sheet arbitrage and fee components of economic performance. Favorable cyclical factors (e.g., low default rates) that enhanced economic performance during the time period referred to in this quote are likely to reverse.

   Financial Darwinism Response: Commercial banks and other depositories must fight for balance sheet arbitrage and grow fee businesses through business strategy and corporate finance activities. Most importantly, they must transition from a buy-and-hold mode of operation to dynamic management of risks on their balance sheets.

$$\text{Dynamic Finance Notation: } r_A - r_L \rightarrow \alpha_{ARB} + \overset{\Rightarrow}{\underset{\Leftarrow}{\sum}} \beta_i P_i + F$$

Using the notations from both the old-world and the risk-based economic performance equations, the previous formula describes the transition from a static to a dynamic business model. As before, dynamic management of systematic risks is depicted through the arrows around the summation sign.

This section reinforces the now-familiar motif: Due to secular pressures faced by traditional financial businesses with static business models, the task of economic value creation by financial institutions has fundamentally changed. Active risk-taking and business model transformations should play an increasingly important role in economic value creation. Strategic vision of financial executives on how to generate economic performance while controlling risk is likely to become a differentiating factor, a determinant of not only success but of the very economic viability of financial institutions in the changed world. Have leading financial firms and institutional investors come to the same conclusion?

Responsive Recalibrations of Business Models

Responsive recalibrations of business models entail the proactive enhancement of the individual components of the risk-based economic performance equation. This is typically achieved through a combination of business strategy, corporate finance, risk management, and investment activities. Table 5.1 shows select publicly known, real-world institutional examples of business model recalibrations.

TABLE 5.1   Real-World Examples of Business Model Recalibrations

EP Component	Type of Enhancement	Institutional Examples
Balance Sheet Arbitrage	Growth of retail deposits and improvements in customer service standards	Wachovia
	Debt product innovation coupled with a proactive expansion of the investor base	The Farm Credit System
Principal Investments	Using the firm's own capital to take stakes in other financial institutions	Bank of America, HSBC, RBS, Allianz, ING
	Expansion of hedge funds into private equity activities and vice versa	The Tudor Group, The Blackstone Group, KKR
Systematic Risks	Expansion of the investment universe and dynamic rebalancing of systematic risks according to economic and market views	PIMCO (as asset manager)
Fees	Growth of asset-management businesses, which may be coupled with principal investments	Goldman Sachs
Expenses	Using mergers and acquisitions to lower the cost of operations	The Bank of New York Mellon
Capital Structure	Innovative uses of hybrid capital securities	US Bancorp State Street Bank
	Accelerated share repurchase programs	Marsh & McLennan

Balance Sheet Arbitrage. Beginning in 2003, *Wachovia Corporation* embarked on a new program with the objective of expanding the branch network as a means of growing the deposit base. In addition, Wachovia set out to improve customer service standards and introduce new incentives at the existing branches and those acquired through M & A. Both endeavors have proven effective in achieving deposit growth targets and improving profitability. According to then-CEO Ken Thompson, "growing deposits is perhaps the most profitable thing that a retail and small business bank can do." In a related example, government-sponsored enterprises in the United States, such as the *Federal Farm Credit System*, are constantly creating new debt structures (debentures, callable bonds, medium-term notes, and prepayment-linked debt instruments) to appeal to an increasingly diverse global investor base in an attempt to maintain and potentially enhance their funding advantage. Sources for all examples in this section can be found in the Notes.[2]

Principal Investments. To alleviate pressures on traditional businesses, financial institutions are increasingly using their own capital to make various private and public market investments. Western financial firms' stakes in Chinese commercial banks represent one of the most publicized (and wildly successful) examples of this kind. As of the end of 2007, Bank of America had a 9 percent stake in China Construction Bank worth close to $20 billion; HSBC had a 17 percent stake in Ping An worth in excess of $17 billion; while the Royal Bank of Scotland had a 4 percent stake in the Bank of China worth $6.5 billion. Other financial institutions with principal investments in China included Allianz, Goldman Sachs, ING, and UBS. In another notable trend, the search for diversification of principal investment platforms both in terms of investments and revenue sources has resulted in hedge funds increasingly expanding their investment universe beyond public markets (stocks, bonds, futures, and currencies) and in private equity firms actively venturing into the hedge fund space. In recent examples of the financial convergence, Cerberus Capital Management (an asset-management company) participated in the Chrysler deal in the capacity of a private equity firm, *The Tudor Group* and *The D. E. Shaw Group* set up private equity units, while *The Blackstone Group* and *KKR Financial Holdings* set up hedge funds.

Dynamic Management of Systematic Risks. An asset-management firm, *PIMCO,* has always been very active in articulating its investment process—particularly as far as dynamic macroeconomic and market views are concerned—when managing its clients' portfolios. Thus, PIMCO uses its *Secular Forum*—a conference consisting of its own professionals and out-side speakers—to analyze such broad trends as those discussed in Chapter 1, subsequently formulating long-term investment decisions. Additionally, a variety of shorter-horizon tactical overlays is constantly applied, as described in the monthly commentaries by its Chief Investment Officer. For example, beginning in 2002 when the Federal Reserve embarked on an interest-rate tightening cycle, PIMCO advocated reducing duration of fixed-income port-folios. In later years, because of the buildup of Chinese and other countries' foreign exchange reserves, the firm took a bearish view on the U.S. dollar. Beginning in 2005, when the monetary tightening in the United States was nearing an end amidst disconcerting news on the inflation front, purchases of Treasury Inflation Protected Securities were advocated. Subsequently, with inflation in the United States remaining moderate, the global economy showing strength, and the U.S. economy slowing, PIMCO favored greater allocations to U.S. Treasuries relative to foreign government bonds. These types of decisions represent the very essence of dynamic rebalancing of systematic risks discussed throughout this book. It is important to reiterate that PIMCO's investment process is related to investing clients' assets as opposed to using its own capital to take views on financial markets.

Fee Businesses. In a move designed to grow fee businesses by leveraging the successful track record of principal investment activities, *Goldman Sachs* made a decision to transfer some of its principal-strategies trading teams from investment bank into the asset-management division. Relocating these businesses was intended to enable capital gathering from outside the firm, resulting in the growth of fee businesses. As an additional benefit—and very much consistent with lessons learned from the financial market crises discussed later in this chapter—this move was designed to give investment professionals more flexibility during market dislocations, forestalling the need to liquidate positions in the face of a liquidity crunch or mark-to-market volatility. Independently, the company announced plans to establish a private equity fund intended to utilize the firm's own capital as well as money from outside sources to take equity stakes in hedge funds. While these examples represent the improvement of the fee-based component of the economic performance equation, they also link fee-based businesses with principal investment activities.

Expense Management. In 2006, *The Bank of New York* announced the acquisition of *Mellon Financial* in a transaction that created *The Bank of New York Mellon*—"the world's largest securities servicing firm," according to the company. Among many expected benefits of the merger were annual cost reductions of about $700 million as the combined workforce was reduced from about 40,000 people to about 36,000 people.

Capital Structure Optimization. Hybrid capital securities (that have the features of both debt and equity instruments) allow modern financial institutions and non-financial corporations to balance regulatory and rating agency considerations while minimizing the total after-tax cost of the capital structure. More specifically, due to tax-deductibility of interest payments, some hybrid debt instruments have a much lower after-tax cost of capital compared to common equity while fulfilling some important regulatory and rating-agency equity requirements. Institutions that have been particularly active in the realm of improving economic performance through cost of capital minimization by actively issuing hybrid capital include *US Bancorp* and *Florida Power and Light*. In certain cases, innovative capital issuance can be coupled with the use of sophisticated financial technologies that allow financial institutions and corporations to purchase their own common stock in tax- and accounting-efficient ways and improve return-on-equity metrics. Notable examples of such accelerated share repurchases include *State Street Bank, Marsh & McLennan,* and a variety of technology companies, with some evidence of a favorable response to these actions by the equity markets.

Real-World Business Model Transformations

In addition to responsive recalibrations directed at improving the individual components of the economic performance equation, modern financial institutions are increasingly embarking on comprehensive business model transformations in order to dynamically create economic value for their stakeholders. Given the lack of relevant financial disclosures, many of these transformations are articulated informally, through interviews of executives, company investor conferences, and other means. Table 5.2 presents a variety of publicly known actions that fall under the umbrella of business model transformations. Many of them appear to be directed at overcoming the challenges facing static business models.

Transition away from static business models via greater allocations to alternative investments. In 2007, the Chinese Government announced its intention to establish a $200 billion investment fund, called the *China Investment Corporation*, designed to earn a higher return on China's foreign-exchange reserves. Officials of the company indicated even before the official launch that the fund intended to allocate capital to alternative investments and equity securities, with multibillion-dollar stakes in the Blackstone Group and Morgan Stanley following in short order. In a series of similar developments, sovereign wealth funds have been gathering alternative assets and company stakes in an attempt to change the buy-and-hold orientation of their business models, as illustrated, for instance, by Abu Dhabi's Investment Authority taking a sizable stake in Citigroup and other similar transactions. In the pension arena, the *Teachers Retirement System of Texas* announced plans to invest as much as one third of its $112 billion in assets in alternative investments. Among university endowments, the *Yale Endowment* is well-known for expanding their portfolio to include alternative investments of as much as 65 percent of its portfolio. Among insurers and reinsurers, *Allstate* allocated significant capital to European private equity and other alternative assets, whereas *SwissRe* bought a 15 percent stake in the British hedge fund Brevan Howard Asset Management in order to "strengthen the reinsurer's position" in "a growing and very attractive sector." Sources for all examples in this section can be found in the Notes.[3]

Transition away from static business models via dynamic management of systematic risks. Wells Fargo has been particularly active in the realm of top-down dynamic management of systematic risks in recent years, as seen from the company's financial disclosures and earnings calls:

> *We take positions based on market expectations or to benefit from price differences between financial instruments and markets, subject to risk limits established and monitored by Corporate ALCO.*

> *. . . After having sold all of our lower-yielding adjustable rate mortgages and securities . . . when long-term interest rates were substantially lower, we increased our investments in longer-term securities as long-term interest rates rose, adding approximately $30 billion in securities at attractive yields.*

TABLE 5.2   Real-World Examples of Business Model Transformations

Financial Sector	Business Model Transformation	Institutional Examples
Central Banks Sovereign Wealth Funds DB Pension Plans College Endowments Insurance Companies	Transition away from static business models via allocations to alternative investments $$r_A - r_L \to \alpha_{PI}$$	China Investment Corp. ADIA Yale Endowment Texas Teachers Swiss Re Allstate
Commercial Banks Insurance Companies Pension Plans	Transition away from static business models via dynamic management of systematic risks $$r_A - r_L \to \overset{\Rightarrow}{\underset{\Leftarrow}{\sum}} \beta_i P_i$$	Wells Fargo MetLife
Insurance Companies Commercial Banks REITs	Transformation of risk-taking businesses into fee-based businesses via securitization $$\sum \beta_i P_i \to F$$	AIG*
Investment Banks	Coupling of strategic advice with financing and principal investment activities $$F \to \alpha_{PI} + \overset{\Rightarrow}{\underset{\Leftarrow}{\sum}} \beta_i P_i + F$$	Goldman Sachs
Commercial Banks Investment Banks	Shorting out-of-the-money options via acquisitions of reinsurance companies or asset strategies $$+ \sum \beta_i P_i$$	Lehman Brothers*
Financial Services	Coupling of brokerage with other fee-based services, such as strategic advice $$F \to F + F$$	Marsh, Inc.

*Important examples despite the companies' problems during the 2007–2008 financial crisis.

. . .We positioned ourselves during the height of the MBS market turmoil to benefit from a flight to quality by holding proportionately more of our economic hedges of the MSR in non-MBS instruments like Treasury futures and options, swaps, and options on swaps. We were able to reverse this positioning and lock in the flight-to-quality gains as the MBS market recovered later.

Meanwhile, a *MetLife* executive attributed a part of the company's stellar investment performance over a certain time period to "big sector calls": capping LBO investments in 2006, selling bonds of General Motors and Ford Motor Co. a month before they were downgraded in 2005, and getting out of the riskiest subprime debt holdings in 2004.

Transformation of risk-taking into fee-based business via securitization. For close to a decade, AIG Risk Finance, a division of the American International Companies, has been using securitization in the risk transfer of policies that combine finite insurance and excess of loss coverage. Through the so-called B FIRST (Blended Finite Insurance and Risk Securitization Transactions) program, corporations, insurance, and reinsurance companies have been afforded a means of integrating risk financing, profit sharing, catastrophic loss protection, and liquidity available through securitization. Under the program, companies obtain the desired protection via insurance or reinsurance policies underwritten by AIG. In turn, a portion of the risk embedded in these policies is transferred to the capital markets via securitization. As AIG's experience in 2007–2008 has shown, this process needs to be accompanied by new-world strategic vision of executives, proper integration of business and risk-taking decisions, and rigorous risk management, as repeatedly emphasized in this book. In other instances, a wide range of financial institutions in the United States adopted the so-called "originate-securitize-and-sell" business models, where pools of mortgage loans were originated internally as well as by third parties and then sold into the capital markets via securitization. In the aftermath of the 2007–2008 credit and liquidity crisis, where the relationship between third-party origination and subsequent credit performance became better understood, origination businesses began to refocus on maintaining the direct contact with their customers. The inherent risks of "originate-securitize-and-sell" business models in environments where structured product markets become debilitated came to the forefront as well, raising a host of business and risk-management issues.

Integration of strategic advice, financing, and principal investment activities. As the secular forces put significant pressures on fee-based businesses across the financial industry, *Goldman Sachs* has responded to compressing fees by integrating several distinct businesses in order to simultaneously (a) compete for advisory businesses by providing one-stop solutions for the firm's clients, as well as (b) enhance the principal investment and systematic risk components of economic performance. In the process, the company set out to become an "advisor, coinvestor, and financier" for its clients. This business model transformation has the following important feature worth noting. In order to win (typically fee-based) customer business, principal investment and systematic risk exposures are taken on. However, if the resulting risks do not adhere to the risk-taking appetite or market views, they can subsequently be eliminated via advanced financial tools such as derivatives hedging. As a perfect case in point, during most of 2007, Goldman Sachs "maintained a net short subprime position with the use of derivatives and therefore stood to benefit from declining prices in the mortgage market." In other words, after all customer-related and other business decisions have been made, a deliberate risk overlay was used to tailor firm-wide systematic risk exposures on the desired levels, appropriately balancing business strategy, corporate finance, and risk-taking decisions.

Shorting options via acquisitions of reinsurance companies and asset strategies. As discussed in Chapter 4, decisions regarding optimal business model mixes often encompass the executives' views on the role of short options in the generation of economic performance. Suggesting the belief that shorting out-of-the-money options would benefit the existing business mix, *Lehman Brothers* acquired a minority interest in Wilton Re, a U.S. mortality risk reinsurer, in 2007, while its U.K. subsidiary, *Libero Ventures,* began offering market making, risk transfer, and securitization services in the P & C reinsurance space. Obviously, as Lehman Brothers' experience has shown, the quest for continuous innovation does not guarantee financial survival if the entire enterprise is not properly risk-managed. In other related examples, many other financial institutions have been shorting out-of-the-money options in various markets via large over-the-counter purchases of range-accrual structured notes and derivatives as part of a deliberate business strategy in the spirit of business model transformations.

Coupling of fee-based services. In 2004, Marsh, Inc., the world's largest insurance broker and a subsidiary of Marsh & McLennan Companies, embarked on a well-publicized business model transformation. Accompanied by the extensive "The Upside of Risk" media campaign, the firm endeavored to leverage its expertise in risk management to couple brokerage and strategic advisory services, both fee-based businesses. According to the company's CEO at the time, the objective was to help the clients "understand the new realities of risks, mitigate them, and turn them into [business or investment] opportunities..." This transformation—designed to introduce new fee-based sources of revenue—generally adhered to the spirit of the *silo busting* framework described by Ranjay Gulati of The Kellogg School of Management.

It is important to acknowledge that active risk taking and business model transformations are double-edged swords. News headlines about investment banks' losses stemming from unhedged "originate-securitize-and-sell" residential mortgage businesses, leveraged loans, as well as various institutions' forays into proprietary trading all serve as examples of economic value destruction rather than value creation. As emphasized repeatedly in the book, dynamic strategic management requires a comprehensive decision-making framework accompanied by the change in the executive skill set, full command of advanced financial tools, as well as rigorous risk-management capabilities. Otherwise, attempts to adapt are likely to have an equally sad ending as the refusals to acknowledge the change and evolve.

Stakeholder Communication & Equity Valuation in a Dynamic World

In the absence of relevant risk-based disclosures, modern financial institutions' communication about successes and failures of dynamic management and business model transformations is often fragmented and anecdotal. As shown earlier, while some relevant information can be distilled from news articles, interviews with executives, annual reports, and earnings releases, the process lacks consistency or rigor. This section departs from the reality on the ground, operating under the assumption that the movement toward risk-focused regulation and fair value accounting will continue. Taken to its natural conclusion (in an admittedly future setting), imagine the world in which relevant information about economic performance, risk-based business models, and risks inherent in financial institutions is available to external stakeholders. If so, how would that impact equity market valuations and the process of shareholder communication?

In a world of dynamic management, proactive stakeholder communication that effectively describes the process of economic value creation is likely to become paramount in shaping capital market perceptions and achieving premium equity market valuation. Of particular complexity and importance here is the increasing contribution of active risk taking to economic performance, which has important (and varying!) implications for financial institutions, lenders, counterparties, regulators, rating agencies, and equity investors. Thus, as financial disclosures gradually enable external stakeholders to measure various risk-based components of economic performance and track their behavior over time, equity valuations should become more directly related to economic performance as opposed to accounting earnings:

Equity Valuation ~ Properties of Economic Performance Over Time

In a parallel to accounting earnings-based price-to-earnings (P/E) ratio, its economic counterpart can be defined as the *price-to-economic performance* ratio:

*Share Price = Economic Performance * Price-to-Economic-Performance Ratio*

In the same way that risk-averse investors assign additional "haircuts" (or risk premia) when discounting riskier future cash flows, lower equity market valuations (P/E ratios) are currently assigned to more complex and opaque businesses (e.g., investment banks) relative to more transparent businesses (e.g., money management firms). As risk-based transparency gradually enables external stakeholders to understand the behavior of economic performance and its components over time, price-to-economic performance ratios—different for each risk-based component of the economic performance equation—should reflect the inherent risk/return characteristics of corresponding risk-based business models. Notice that discussing equity valuation multiples in terms of risk-based components of economic performance is arguably more straightforward than dealing with traditionally defined business segments since the latter may encompass multiple business models and overlapping risk exposures. The numerical example of the relationship between risk-based economic performance, transparency, and equity market valuations is presented in Appendix B.

As an illustration, consider the following observation: Investment banks' price-to-earnings ratios have declined over time as the proportion of revenues from trading and principal investing activities increased.[4] The natural implication of this statement is that equity market valuation ratios corresponding to principal investment businesses of broker/dealers are lower than those on traditional investment banking businesses such as M & A advisory, underwriting, or brokerage. Higher inherent risk and lack of transparency to external stakeholders are among the reasons for lower multiples corresponding to revenues from these businesses, with accounting earnings currently serving as a best-available proxy for economic performance.

Not surprisingly, not all sources of economic performance are created equal: Enterprises with a high proportion of economic performance due to balance sheet arbitrage or sustainable fee-generating activities are likely to be valued at a premium relative to institutions whose economic performance comes primarily from principal investment activities and systematic risk exposures. In a side note, the observed behavior of equity valuations, analyst reports, and news headlines suggest that implicit equity valuation multiples corresponding to various components of economic performance may be financial-sector specific and vary over time. In addition to general level of risk-aversion, valuation multiples are often reflective of the degree of stakeholders' comfort with an institutions' involvement in riskier or "nontraditional" businesses. In this regard, the perceived risk-management capabilities, skills of the personnel, and other management aspects all play an important role. For instance, investment banks with successful track records of principal investment activities often enjoy premium valuations relative to their industry peers. Due to investment banks being at the center of financial innovation, investors have not seemed to mind—and often encouraged—risk-taking behavior provided that state-of-the-art risk-management capabilities and rigorous compliance controls appeared to be in place.[5] In other cases, however, stakeholders and regulators did get visibly concerned about concentrated systematic risk exposures (think of Mortgage Partnership Finance programs of Federal Home Loan Banks) or business model transformations out of traditional static businesses into principal investing activities without requisite capabilities.

In the world of dynamic management, equity market valuations of financial institutions are likely to be more directly linked to economic performance and underlying risk-based business models. The following factors should become particularly important.

- *Consistent and growing economic performance over time.* As components of economic performance and their histories become available through updated financial disclosures, a variety of performance attribution and econometric analyses will become useful in analyzing the properties of economic performance over time.[6] The consistency in economic value creation is likely to become a contributor to achieving premium equity valuation. Analogously to the case of accounting earnings, accelerating trends in the absolute as well as risk-adjusted economic performance time series should ultimately translate into the expansion of price-to-economic performance ratios. The track record of economic value creation through active business model transformations, including dynamic management of systematic risks, should become particularly important in this regard.
- *Growth of fee-based businesses and preservation of balance sheet arbitrage.* These components of economic performance appear to be viewed favorably by the equity markets at the time when this book is written. Therefore, growing the proportion of economic performance due to fees and balance sheet arbitrage—which can be demonstrated through economic performance attribution—is likely to translate into premium equity valuations.
- *Proactive stakeholder communication and education.* When financial institutions behave more dynamically, perceptions of their future prospects are shaped by the communication between executive management and stakeholders more than ever before. Several important aspects of this communication are important. First, the strategic vision of executives as well as their rationale for business model transformations and active risk-taking decisions need to be described. Second, applicable track records of successfully translating competitive advantages and dynamic management into consistent performance need to be

communicated. Third, the presence of necessary skills and advanced capabilities needs to be demonstrated to stakeholders. All three should be particularly important for improving valuation multiples on the revenues from principal investment activities as well as dynamic management of systematic risks. Thus, for principal activities to be a significant part of an institution's earnings and not attract a sizable equity valuation discount, the portfolio of principal investment activities—proprietary trading, private equity investments, stakes in hedge funds, and so on—should be perceived as well-diversified, with sophisticated risk controls in place. In terms of dynamic management of systematic risks, a rigorous top-down investment process, advanced asset/liability management and enterprise risk-management capabilities, proven skills of the executive team, and a long successful track record are likely to be prerequisites to a premium equity valuation. Notice that the latter task is no different from asset managers' interactions with investors where results of active beta management are articulated through return attribution analyses as well as descriptions of the underlying investment philosophy and process. Of course, in the case of financial institutions communicating with the capital markets, the audience and the language are different, the setting is more complex, and the potential impact of inadequate communication on equity valuations is high.

Strategic flexibility, innovation, robust mixes of risk-based businesses, full utilization of all advanced frameworks and tools, state-of-the-art risk management and controls, and proactive stakeholder communication that articulates the rationale and track record of active risk-taking decisions and business model transformations are likely to become critical ingredients of achieving premium equity valuation in the dynamic new world.

Economic Value Creation (and Destruction) by Non-Financial Corporations

So far in this book, the risk-based economic performance equation has been primarily applied to economic value creation by financial institutions. In this section, I briefly discuss the implications of risk-based economic performance for non-financial corporations, where links between economic value creation, executive choices, and risk management are also important in a variety of business activities, including debt issuance, capital structure optimization, pension plan management, securitization, and M & A.

Consider responsive recalibrations of business models in the context of non-financial corporations. In terms of similarities with financial institutions, growing fee-based businesses, minimizing expenses, and optimizing the capital structure to reduce the overall cost of capital are examples of actions by non-financial corporations where individual components of the risk-based economic performance equation can be proactively enhanced. There are, of course, important differences. For instance, balance sheet arbitrage and principal investment activities typically do not apply to non-financial corporations, whereas economic performance due to non-financial activities is an added dimension that is beyond the scope of this work.

As in the case of financial institutions, active risk taking—including the dynamic management of systematic risks—is becoming an important component of economic performance of non-financial corporations. In fact, these firms routinely take on financial risks in their normal course of business:

- International operations result in foreign currency exposures.
- Debt issuance and capital structure optimization lead to interest rate and yield curve exposures.
- Financing activities and securitization may change balance sheet exposures to a plethora of market, credit, liquidity, and funding risks.
- Pension plan management and certain M & A transactions often entail equity, commodity, interest rate, credit, and other risks.

The following brief discussion on earnings volatility and occasional outright losses of non-financial corporations demonstrates the important role that the management of systematic risks plays in the lives of non-financial corporations. Recall some of the notable negative news headlines over the past few years. Foreign exchange–related losses were one of the key factors in Four Seasons Hotels' earnings disappointment and subsequent fall in stock valuation in the third quarter of 2005. Abitibi Consolidated grew sales but took a sizable after-tax loss due to foreign exchange charges in the second quarter of 2004, with share prices declining by more than 15 percent in the aftermath. In the fourth quarter of 2006, SAP's earnings disappointed in large part due to foreign exchange losses, leading to over 10 percent share price declines following the earnings announcement. In late 2007 to early 2008, ADC Telecommunications, 3M, Ciena, Bristol-Myers, Lawson Software, and even Apex Silver Mines (a silver producer in Bolivia, Peru, and Mexico) all reported write downs related to the so-called auction rate securities that were used in cash management. Some of these investments—deemed *conservative* due to their AAA and AA credit ratings—were backed by subprime mortgages and, hence, were exposed to a number of systematic and security-specific risks.[7]

In an attempt to generalize from these examples, Table 5.3 presents the following classification of executive actions, implicit risk-taking philosophies, and risk-management practices of non-financial corporations.

TABLE 5.3   Executive Decisions and Risk Management at Non-Financial Corporations

Category	Interpretation & Comments	Economic Value Implications
Risk exposures are misunderstood or ineffectively managed.	Risk-management failure.	Usually Value Destructive
Risk exposures are understood and largely hedged out.	Typically a conservative choice that limits both the upside and the downside in earnings. In some cases, hedging that leverages business synergies can be value-added.	Value-Neutral and Potentially Value-Added
Risk exposures are understood but deliberately left unhedged.	Philosophical risk-taking decision on the CEO/CFO/Board of Directors level. Requires a justification that (a) the compensation for bearing systematic risks is adequate and shareholder value-added, (b) this is a desirable use of capital, and (c) the firm is able to bear this level and type of risk.	?
Risk exposures are understood and dynamically managed over time.	An integrated, top-down ALCO process that takes active views on systematic risks to create economic value. Activities include debt issuance, foreign currency management, and pension plans. Risk management is performed using an "optimal" combination of financial and operational tools.	Potentially Value-Added

Not surprisingly, risk is one of the key dimensions in Table 5.3, suggesting that as business decisions are being made, risk-management implications need to be explicitly articulated. For instance, what is the foreign currency risk associated with substituting a domestic supplier with an international one? What is the impact on balance sheet yield curve and interest-rate risks of issuing a 2-year debenture as opposed to a 10-year callable debt instrument? What is the interest-rate risk associated with a decision of issuing hybrid capital in order to buy back common equity? What is the implication for the enterprise-wide exposures when a pension plan is making a strategic asset reallocation out of equities into hedge funds? All of these decisions involve systematic risks, and their impact on economic value is captured in the corresponding component of the risk-based economic performance equation.

According to Table 5.3, once basic risk-measurement questions are answered, risk management and the strategic vision of executives become inextricably linked. If the management of a corporation believes that it is not in the business of taking on systematic risks, the latter need to be hedged out in the most effective fashion using the universe of advanced financial tools shown in Figure 4.3. If the management endeavors to create additional economic value through dynamic management of systematic risks, then necessary skills, tools, and capabilities must be present. Finally, if a static business model is advocated where systematic risks are understood but carried on the books in an unmanaged fashion, then the rationale for this decision—and its implications related to capital management, earnings volatility, and risk of a financial demise—needs to be rigorously analyzed and explained to the stakeholders.

Executive-level risk-taking decisions are bound to play an increasingly important role in the lives of financial institutions and non-financial corporations alike, significantly affecting economic value creation and equity market valuations.[8]

The Infamous "Carry Trade" and the Old Ways of Thinking

I now return to the topic of the carry trades that represent one of the most blatant examples of the old way of thinking and the dangers it poses in the dynamic new world. Note that the placement of this section near the end of the book is deliberate. First, we are now fully equipped to discuss carry trades from the viewpoint of static business models, risk-based economic performance, and business model transformations. Second, this subject is a perfect prelude to the discussion on modern financial crises presented in the next section.

Our readers might have guessed by now that the old banker joke in Chapter 1 deals with one of the most notorious investment constructs and pieces of the Wall Street jargon—the *carry trade*. Carry trades entail an investor or a financial institution borrowing money relatively "cheaply" and either lending out the funds at higher rates or investing them in higher-yielding securities, pocketing the profit. Notice that the language of this entire discussion—dealing with the differential between assets and liabilities—is an artifact of static business models and the mental paradigm represented by the old-regime economic performance equation.

The deceiving ease with which earnings or returns can be delivered through carry trades is deeply ingrained in the minds of investors and other finance professionals across financial sectors. Banks, insurance companies, real estate investment trusts, money managers, and investment banks all think about certain activities or parts of their businesses as carry trades. There are also examples of carry trades in unexpected settings. Thus, in the world of static asset allocations, where defined benefit pension plans are mostly invested in equities, their asset/liability positioning can be thought of as a carry trade between assets (equities) and liabilities (fixed income), which we have referred to as equity risk premium earlier in the book (Tables 2.1. and 2.2.). Certain funding decisions by non-financial corporations (e.g., issuing long-term debt in periods of steep yield curves and swapping it into floating via interest-rate derivatives) are often also inspired by the carry trades mentality, even though this particular circumstance only includes the liability side of the balance sheet. Note that while debt issuance choices by non-financial corporations where risk-management implications are misunderstood can indeed be characterized as carry trades, this should be distinguished from funding decisions that have a deliberate additional objective of creating economic value through dynamic management of systematic risks—a new frontier for non-financial corporations.

The term itself—*carry trade*—is very visual: While the asset is being simply "carried" on the books—without any hedging or dynamic management—the owner has the privilege of receiving the difference between the asset's yield and the cost of funds. The description appears to casually suggest that the difference in asset/liability returns is effectively an *arbitrage*, a *riskless profit* one receives for simply being a financial intermediary or an investor who has discovered an instance of market inefficiency.

With the help of the risk-based economic performance equation, it can be shown that not all carry trades are created equal. Thus, in circumstances where a significant portion of the yield spread between assets and liabilities is due to balance sheet arbitrage (as it is often the case for commercial banks and government-sponsored enterprises), characterizing this situation as a carry trade may be defensible. In that setting, sustaining and growing static business models (or carry trades) in order to create economic value becomes a dominant objective usually pursued through business strategy and corporate finance activities.

Apart from these rare exceptions, however, most institutional investors and financial institutions do not enjoy balance sheet arbitrage, which makes thinking of carry trades as arbitrage opportunities or *clipping the coupon* especially dangerous. In fact, the *lower* the proportion of economic performance due to balance sheet arbitrage vis-à-vis principal activities and systematic risks (which can be revealed through economic performance attribution), the more *inappropriate* it is to think about such investments or balance sheets as carry trades. In fact, funding and market risks of a retail-funded institution can be substantially different from those of a wholesale-funded institution—precisely because of the balance sheet arbitrage component of economic performance. By implication, the two are likely to have very different equity valuation multiples, as illustrated by a 59 percent decline in E-Trade shares on November 12, 2007 followed by a research report that highlighted the company's reliance on wholesale funding and uninsured deposits.[9]

More often than not, positive carry is a market-based compensation for assuming a variety of systematic and idiosyncratic risks, which corresponds to entirely different components of the economic performance equation—namely, principal investments and systematic risks. For instance, the A/L spread associated with the much-written-about "yen carry trades" was the compensation for foreign exchange and interest-rate risks. On the other hand, "issue commercial paper in Germany to buy U.S. subprime mortgages" carry trades that took center stage during the 2007 to 2008 financial crisis entailed most types of risks known to man: interest rate, yield curve, foreign exchange, credit, prepayment, implied volatility, funding, liquidity, and model risks.[10] Certainly a far cry from a riskless profit!

In more recent examples, the rise of the so-called structured investment vehicles (SIVs) and asset-backed commercial paper (ABCP) conduits represented one of the most palpable examples of leveraged carry trades in an environment of declining investment returns and margin pressures. As per Figure 5.1, the rise in the amount of ABCP outstanding between 2005 and 2007 coincided with the significant flattening of the yield curve (Figure 5.1). Both followed the margin compression of commercial banks (Figure 2.10) and the general decline in risk premia (Figure 3.1). Loading up on carry trades that entailed credit, prepayment, funding, and liquidity risks was exactly the wrong response to pressures. However, the appeal of conduit management fees for commercial banks—coupled with the need for earnings on the part of the conduit and SIV owners—was too strong. In an additional nuance, ABCP conduits were off-balance-sheet liabilities of commercial banks that were not adequately captured by modern financial disclosures, reinforcing the need for risk-based transparency of modern financial institutions.

From the viewpoint of *Dynamic Finance*, most carry trades represent static business models whose underlying risks are obscured by the old way of thinking. From properties of static business models as well as institutional experiences, it follows that whenever risk premia decline, static business models where a predefined level of returns between assets and liabilities results needs to be maintained irrespective of the external environment's lead to progressively greater risk-taking. The outcome? In the words of Alan Greenspan, "history has not dealt kindly with the aftermath of protracted

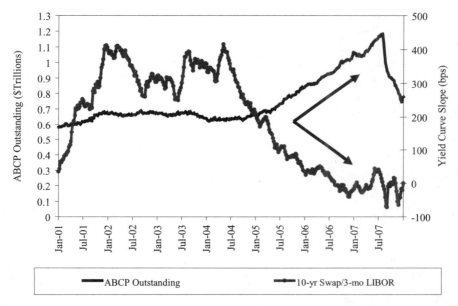

FIGURE 5.1 Asset-Backed Commercial Paper Outstanding (2001–2007)
Source: Bloomberg, FRB.

periods of low risk premiums," which is especially relevant to static business models and carry trades. Magazine articles with stories of once-successful investors—who in the spirit of *Fooled by Randomness* "borrowed from the future," subsequently lost money, and then had to sell their luxury yachts with names like *Positive Carry*—speak for themselves.

In the new dynamic world, risk-management sophistication will increasingly determine investment performance and economic value creation. Departing from the old way of thinking illustrated by carry trades and focusing on the active management of risks underlying investment strategies, portfolios, and entire balance sheets is the first step in the right direction.

A Dynamic Finance Perspective on Modern Financial Crises

Witch Hunts

In the book *Risk Management,* published in the aftermath of the 1998 LTCM market crisis, Dr. Bennett Golub and I observed that renewed interest in risk management typically follows large shocks to the financial system and the subsequent negative headlines. Media storms, financial ruin, and notable executive departures that accompanied major market dislocations of the past decade—most importantly the 1998 LTCM and the 2007–2008 financial crises—were a vivid illustration of this phenomenon. The latter episode is especially instructive. Prior to 2007, the stage for the crisis was dramatically set by the market tranquility and the complacency of investors and executives during this especially peculiar period of the Great Moderation. The ferocity and the magnitude of the dislocation that followed posed a sharp contrast to the preceding environment.

Experience has shown that once market crises subside, dust settles, and the investment climate reverts to relative business-as-usual, then attention shifts to retrospection and lessons learned. In this regard, unique features of a particular crisis are identified and distinguished from characteristics that are common to most modern dislocations, such as flights to quality, volatility, illiquidity, inability to borrow, the breakdown in "normal" relationships between asset classes, and so on. Such analyses have important implications for executive decisions, risk management, investment strategy, public policy, and regulation.

Using the 2007–2008 market dislocation as a case study, this section uses the risk-based economic equation to analyze the dominant features of modern financial crises from the perspective of *Dynamic Finance* as follows:

- demonstrating how the interaction of secular and period-specific forces may amplify leverage and risk taking beyond the cyclical phenomena
- explaining the endogenous mechanics of market dislocations by separating their unique characteristics from those common to other market crises
- revealing how pressures on static business models can contribute to winding up the financial crises, thus generalizing the institutional examples from Chapter 2
- cautioning against vicious circles of risk taking that can lead to systemic global financial shocks

The Vicious Circle of Leverage and Risk Taking

Analysts and regulators have long argued that "the primary cause of financial instability has always been, and will continue to be, overextension in risk-taking and balance sheets, i.e., the occasional build-up in financial imbalances that at some point unwind."[11] Such cyclical behavior is always a good place to start: Long periods of economic expansion and low default rates do tend to result in looser underwriting standards, plentiful access to cheap credit, or less onerous covenants of debt instruments. I argue, however, that viewing the 2007–2008 dislocation simply as a cyclical credit phenomenon is limiting. What were the additional factors that caused an unprecedented

buildup in system-wide leverage? What was the role of alternative investment vehicles, structured products, and derivatives? How did the globalization of capital markets, disintermediation, and margin pressures contribute
to both the winding up and the unwinding of the crisis? What were the
roles of pensions, investment banks, and other financial institutions? Revisiting the risk-based economic performance equation in the context of the
macroeconomic and financial market environment that preceded that financial crisis provides insights into these questions.

1. Due to disintermediation, greater availability of financial information,
   increased competition, greater consumer sophistication, and other secular forces, fees associated with basic financial intermediation activities
   have experienced a dramatic compression.
2. The same set of forces simultaneously put pressures on the balance
   sheet arbitrage component of economic performance.
3. As an immediate (defensive) reaction to both, executives dispatched a
   variety of corporate finance activities in order to preserve balance sheet
   arbitrage, reduce expenses, and optimize capital structures. Growth of
   fee-based businesses (e.g., asset management) became an important
   part of supplementing existing sources of earnings.
4. When in many cases that did not prove to be sufficient to counteract
   margin and fee compression trends, institutional investors and financial
   institutions turned to greater risk taking en masse. That included top-
   level active management of systematic risks on an enterprise-wide level
   as well as principal investment activities, both of which I examine in
   more detail below.

Systematic risk taking. As balance sheet arbitrage and fees declined,
financial institutions and investors increasingly took on systematic risks in
an attempt to deliver earnings and investment returns. Carry trades, selling
options, explicit leverage, and increasingly complex and opaque financial
instruments and derivatives (e.g., collateralized debt obligations involving
subprime mortgages) were all used in this regard. Meanwhile, due to cyclical
(e.g., low volatility and low default rates) and period-specific (e.g., over-
seas demand for U.S. assets) factors, interest rates and risk premia across
asset classes were on a decline as well. The vicious circle thus ensued:
Compressing returns and risk premia resulted in larger risk taking which, in
turn, compressed risk premia further (Figure 5.2).

Principal Investment Activities. Simultaneously, financial institutions and
institutional investors turned to proprietary trading, hedge funds, and private
equity firms in search for returns, diversification of revenue sources, or
both. Given increased capital market efficiency and large pools of money
chasing the same universe of financial assets, opportunities for delivering

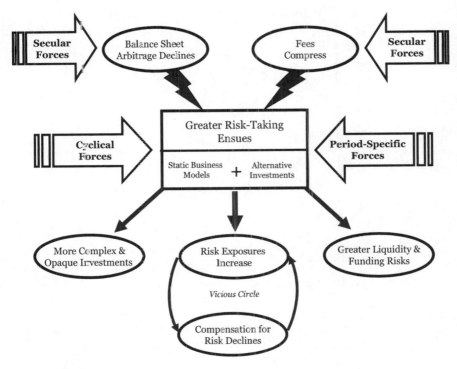

FIGURE 5.2 The Vicious Circle of Risk-Taking and Leverage

pure alpha declined significantly, making proprietary desks and hedge funds turn to systematic risks for sources of returns. This additionally compressed risk premia and contributed to the vicious circle. Meanwhile, private equity firms exacerbated the leverage in the system via leveraged buyouts.

Of crucial importance, what in retrospect clearly appears to have been greater risk taking, was not perceived as such by many market participants during the leverage buildup. On the contrary, as market volatility and risk premia declined, so did the estimates of Value-at-Risk and other risk measures. This shortcoming of some risk-management methodologies—their reliance on short recent history in estimating ex ante risk—has proven to be a particularly dangerous practice capable of exacerbating financial crises, re-enforcing the need for stress testing.

Understanding mechanisms and implications of financial instability involves, among other things, modeling the "endogenous nature of the processes through which financial imbalances build up and unwind."[12] *Dynamic Finance* does precisely that by illuminating how the interaction of secular, cyclical, and period-specific forces amplified leverage and risk taking in the prelude to the 2007–2008 credit and liquidity crisis, which

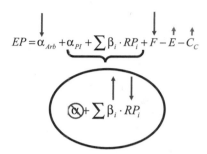

FIGURE 5.3 The Relationship Between Secular Trends, Risk Premia, and Leverage

is illustrated in Figures 5.2 and 5.3. The impact of these forces on the individual components of risk-based economic performance is shown in Figure 5.3. Balance sheet arbitrage and fees declined. Expense management, capital structure optimization, and new sources of fees failed to make up for the lost earnings. Greater risk taking—through principal investment or top-down systematic risk-taking activities—resulted in increasingly leveraged institutions and investors chasing the same pool of assets, compressing risk premia, and assuming ever-greater risks and leverage. Interestingly, a *Financial Times* article argued at the time that "systemic risk in the hedge-fund industry may have increased."[13] In reality, the issue was significantly larger in scope: Systematic risk taking by all market participants—investors, financial institutions, and non-financial corporations—has increased dramatically.

The Vicious Circle of Deleveraging

While not all market crises may have an identifiable catalyst, both the 1998 and 2007–2008 episodes were sparked by well-publicized exogenous events. In 1998, it was Russia's default on its sovereign debt. In 2007, it was housing market deterioration in the United States, accompanied by the increase in delinquencies on subprime mortgages. Interestingly, once a catalyst spikes risk aversion and starts wide-spread deleveraging, significant dislocations of the past decade have exhibited the following common behavior graphically shown in Figure 5.4.[14]

- As risk-aversion increases, investors and financial institutions try to reduce total risk per unit of capital and/or raise cash to cover margin calls.
- More complex positions experience significant price declines on very thin or no trading as well as lack of liquidity. "Securitize-and-sell" business models become incapacitated.
- As forced liquidations and deleveraging intensify, illiquidity of complex instruments results in liquid positions being sold regardless of the

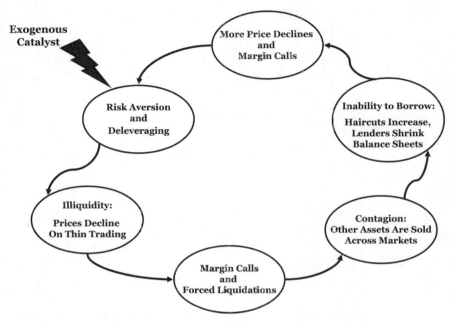

FIGURE 5.4 The Deleveraging Stage of a Modern Financial Crisis

market they are in. This phenomenon (typically referred to as *contagion* and illustrated in Fig. 5.5) tends to increase correlations among asset classes that may be fundamentally uncorrelated. The effect of subprime developments on corporate credit markets in 2007 to 2008 and the impact of Russia's default on commercial mortgage-backed securities in 1998 (now shown) are well-known examples of this behavior.

- Prime brokers increase haircuts on leveraged positions, forcing additional liquidations. This further depresses the value of securities, exacerbating margin calls. In this regard, business models and risk-management practices that protect institutions from being a forced seller in times of crisis prove to be a major competitive advantage (just think of university endowments, sovereign wealth funds, pension plans, and retail-funded banks).
- Dealers become reluctant to take positions of any significant size and widen bid/ask spreads.
- Commercial and investment banks pare down lending activities due to risk aversion as well as contingent liabilities, and it becomes difficult to obtain financing in the capital markets for all participants. By some estimates, between the end of July and the beginning of October 2007 in the United States alone, large commercial banks were forced to put on

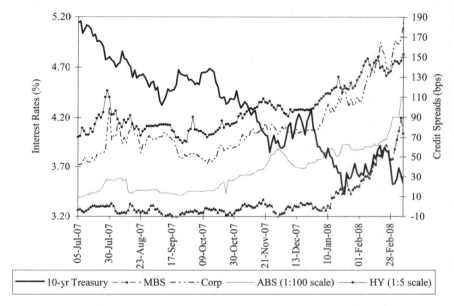

FIGURE 5.5 Contagion and Flight-to-Quality During the 2007–2008 Market Crisis

Source: Bloomberg, Bear Stearns.

Note: MBS = Mortgage/LIBOROAS; HY = high yield 5-year OTR CDS;
Corp IG = IG CDS; ABS = ABS BBB CDS

their balance sheets close to $280 billion in LBO loans and commercial
paper-related commitments.

- If debt markets can be accessed at all, borrowers have to move away
  from the commercial paper market and issue term debt, with attendant
  derivatives hedging sending ripple effects across financial markets. Additionally, new types of derivatives may exacerbate the volatility of market movements, revealing supply-and-demand discrepancies between
  derivatives and cash markets.
- Dominant regulatory frameworks and similarities in both risk exposures
  and risk-management practices across financial institutions become the
  determining factor during this unwinding stage of market crises, overwhelming macroeconomic backdrops. This has prompted observers to
  describe certain aspects of such crises as *technical* (related to supply-
  and-demand) rather than *fundamental* (related to macroeconomics)
  phenomena.
- During the periods of high risk-aversion and illiquidity, the lack of transparency associated with modern financial institutions and dependence
  on capital market funding significantly increase the costs of financial
  distress. Forced liquidations of securities take place at price levels that

are significantly lower than intrinsic values. Simultaneously, counterparties stop doing business with firms whose viability is in doubt, greatly exacerbating the types of vicious circles described in Figure 5.4.

The Complex, Opaque, and Interconnected World

Financial market dislocations witnessed over recent decades are indicative of the increased complexity and interconnectivity of the global financial system. In fact, rapid innovation, increased efficiency, and globalization of financial markets have all amplified the ferocity of vicious circles observed during market crises:

- In an attempt to counteract compressing margins and lower returns, investors and financial institutions invest in progressively complex securities with nontransparent structures and misunderstood underlying risks.
- Increased complexity and lack of transparency applies not only to financial products but also to financial institutions themselves. Inadequate disclosures create stakeholder and lender uncertainty about risk exposures and contingent liabilities, crippling investment and financing activities in times of crisis.
- Non-risk-based constructs—such as credit ratings and accounting earnings—that attempt to filter out complexity without revealing the true nature of underlying risks and business models—prove not only unhelpful but blinding, exacerbating the vicious circles during both the winding-up as well as unwinding stages.
- "Originate, securitize, and sell" business models that detach originators from credit risk sometimes contribute to the loosening of underwriting standards beyond cyclical factors.[15]

Secular margin and fee compression, complex investment products, naïve (or improperly incentivised) investors, and opaque financial institutions make a dangerous combination, particularly when period-specific forces amplify the already-abundant peak-of-the-cycle liquidity, contributing to the mispricing of risk premia.

Unintended Consequences of Globalization and Financial Innovation

Earlier in this book, I outlined important secular trends relevant to financial institutions. Capital markets and financial services have become increasingly globalized and integrated with real economies. Financial innovation has allowed increasingly specific risks to be modeled, isolated, and traded. Securitization revolutionized the way many financial institutions access capital markets, leading to new types of complex financial instruments. As a net result, financial risks become dispersed around the world in the most sophisticated and opaque ways. While this is generally considered a net positive in terms of risk-adjusted allocation of capital and greater potential for risk management by individual investors and financial institutions, recent experiences suggest that unintended consequences of globalization and financial innovation may arise, especially during market dislocations. In particular, the global diffusion of risks—coupled with the lack of adequate risk-based financial disclosures and faulty regulatory regimes—can dramatically amplify the vicious circles of risk taking as well as deleveraging. The extreme risk aversion on the part of lenders and investors in times of crisis stems from their inability to manage credit and counterparty risks due to the lack of transparency. When a large loss, a forced liquidation, or a default may come from any financial institution or investor worldwide, it serves as a true testament to the increased complexity, interconnectivity, and opaquness of the dynamic new world.

Other Implications and Lessons Learned

From the *Dynamic Finance* perspective, lessons learned from major market crises over the past decade reinforce the main themes of this book.

The need for dynamic management of business models of financial institutions and investment portfolios is self-evident. Due to secular trends, an increasing proportion of economic performance of financial institutions and institutional investors is likely to be driven by active risk taking as opposed to market-insensitive fees or balance sheet arbitrage. Therefore, economic peformance of static business models is likely to become increasingly cyclical, with earnings and returns progressively at the mercy of market environments.

Economic performance expectations—and attendant risk tolerance—have to be explicitly placed in the context of the prevailing economic and market environment. In periods of lower returns and compressed risk premia, financial institutions and institutional investors have to choose between (a) accepting lower returns and earnings, (b) employing increased leverage and more complex products while maintaining static business models, or (c) using dynamic management and business model transformation to combat margin and earnings pressures. Circumstances in which the first choice is made are exceptionally rare given typical incentives of investors and executives. Pressures to deliver growing earnings/returns across all market environments—coupled with similar exposures and risk-management practices across market participants—suggest that vicious circles of leverage and risk taking are likely to occur periodically in the future, most likely toward the end of economic expansions.

Business strategy and corporate finance are poor substitutes for risk-taking decisions. Business strategy, corporate finance, investment decisions, and risk management need to be properly integrated under the umbrella of executive decision making. For instance, a loan originator with a superior client service, excellent underwriting, and premier brand is not immune to ruin if it is simultaneously unable to securitize loans and obtain funding.

Systemic financial crises are the permanent feature of the dynamic new world. In light of the secular forces at play and the increased reliance of financial institutions on active risk taking, insights into the mechanisms according to which market imbalances wind up and subsequently unwind suggest that periodic systemic financial crises à la 1998 and 2007–2008 may be unavoidable, which suggests the need for early detection systems of financial crises as well as investor education.

Beyond the Façade: The Need for Risk-Based Transparency

The lack of transparency associated with modern financial institutions has become indisputable in recent years. It applies to firms that engage in dynamic risk taking and business model transformations in order to create economic value. It also applies to institutions that continue to cling onto static business models, often responding to margin and fee pressures with increased leverage and investments in complex and opaque financial instruments. Inadequate financial disclosures and lack of risk-based transparency tend to result in significant stakeholder and lender uncertainty during financial market dislocations, crippling investment and financing activities. Thus, during recent market dislocations, multihundred-billion dollars in contingent liabilities, writedowns associated with complex instruments, unhedged warehousing and underwriting activities, and proprietary trading losses across a wide range of institutions genuinely surprised capital markets, credit rating agencies, and regulators alike. Importantly, they illustrated once again that actual business models and risk exposures of financial institutions are not always visible to external stakeholders.

Figure 5.6 schematically illustrates this phenomenon using buildings' façades as metaphors for perceptions of financial institutions by external observers. Modern financial disclosures are anchored in the language of flows of funds as opposed to risk-based terms.[16] This is depicted on the left-hand side of the figure, where the legacy business model is described through income and balance sheet statements. The mechanism of funds and products entering, passing through (being transformed), and exiting via various products and services is thus articulated. In a static world, this information may perhaps be adequate to describe a financial institution's business model and its inherent structural risk exposures—direct consequences of the intermediation role or charter.

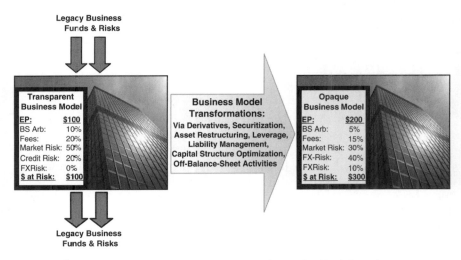

FIGURE 5.6 Business Model Transformations and the Lack of Risk-Based
Transparency

Such a depiction may, however, be not only incomplete but outright
blinding in understanding modern realities. In addition to holding obscure
financial instruments on their balance sheets, today's financial institutions
increasingly use dynamic management, derivatives, structured products, securitization, liability management strategies, and other tools from Figure 4.6
to continuously alter risk/return profiles of balance sheets. Systematic risks
may be recalibrated in an effort to eliminate undesired exposures and enhance risk-adjusted economic performance.[17] Entire business models may
become radically transformed to reflect the strategic vision of the executives on what constitutes an "optimal" collection of risk-based businesses.
In the example depicted in Figure 5.6, the legacy business model of a hypothetical financial institution is transformed through a variety of advanced
financial tools. In the process, *ex ante* economic performance ("EP") and
risk ("$ at Risk") are increased two- and three-fold, respectively, while eco-
nomic performance attribution (relative contributions of various risk-based
components) is changed materially as well: Currency risk is added, the relative importance of market vis-à-vis credit risks is reversed, and the role
of balance sheet arbitrage is diminished. *Thus, the risks inherent in a financial institution—and the very process of economic value creation—has
been changed, yet the perceptions of stakeholders (the façades of the building) have remained the same!* Naturally, this puts the effectiveness of credit
ratings, equity valuations, and analyst reports in doubt.

As business model recalibrations and transformations become increasingly prevalent and frequent in the future, the need for risk-based
transparency—direct, clear, and comprehensive descriptions of financial
intermediaries' business models, risk exposures, and economic value

generation mechanism—is going to become increasing paramount. Examples of how risk-based transparency can be achieved via the risk-based economic performance equation and modern risk management are presented in Appendix B.

Conclusion

By way of summarizing the framework of ideas designed to help financial institutions adapt to the ongoing tectonic shift and succeed through the new kind of strategic vision, Table 5.4 presents a side-by-side comparison of the old regime and the dynamic new world.

TABLE 5.4   The Old Regime vis-à-vis the Dynamic New World

	The Old Regime	The Dynamic New World
The World	Relatively closed economies; less efficient, less developed, and less interconnected financial markets	Globalized, deregulated, and efficient financial markets pervasively integrated with real economies
Macroeconomic Environment	Periods of significant inflation; opaque monetary policies; greater volatility of output, employment, and interest rates	Inflation targeting; more transparent monetary policies; longer periods of economic stability and milder output fluctuations
Compensation for Basic Financial Services	Generous	Much lower and persistently declining
Financial Market Environments	Interest rates and risk premia are relatively high on average	Interest rates and risk premia are lower on average
Financial Crises	Localized, cyclical phenomena exacerbated by lack of risk-management sophistication	Global systemic crises characterized by vicious circles of risk taking and subsequent deleveraging
Basic Financial Information	Significant informational asymmetries	Greater availability of information
Business Models	**Static** (no dynamic risk taking or business model transformations)	**Dynamic** (risk taking is dynamic; business models are transformed with increasing speed and frequency *according to strategic vision*)

(Continued)

TABLE 5.4 (Continued)

	The Old Regime	The Dynamic New World
Description of Business Models	Business segments	Risk-based business models
Drivers of Economic Performance	***Differential returns between static assets and liabilities plus fees minus expenses minus the cost of capital***	***Balance sheet arbitrage, principal investment activities, systematic risks, fees, cost-control, and capital structure optimization***
Economic Performance Equation	$R_A - R_L + F - E - C_C$	$\alpha_{Arb} + \alpha_{PI} + \sum \beta_i \cdot RP_i + F - E - C_C$
Management Focus	Generate stable and growing accounting earnings by growing a robust mix of static businesses	Continually transform and optimize enterprises; maximize absolute and risk-adjusted economic performance
Pillars of Decision Making	Business strategy combined with corporate finance; accounting earnings	Business strategy combined with corporate finance; risk management; investment analysis; accounting earnings
Arsenal of Tools	Leverage, M & A, business strategy	Asset management, securitization, derivatives hedging, debt and capital optimization, M & A, business strategy
Decision-Making Language	Accounting earnings	Risk management
Measures of Performance	Accounting earnings and related metrics: ROA, ROE, ROIC	Absolute and risk-adjusted economic performance
Measures of Risk	Earnings volatility and credit ratings	Economic capital and modern risk measures
Role of Risk Management	Passive and policing	Strategic, proactive, and value-added
Accounting	GAAP	Fair valuation
Regulation	Charter-based	Risk-focused

Financial Darwinism

Executive Action Plan

1. **STRATEGIC VISION**
   (CEO, Board of Directors, Executive Committee)
   a. Define the business mission and stakeholder value proposition.
   b. Describe institutional legacy and competitive advantages.
   c. Evolve and grow champion businesses.
   d. Formulate product, customer, and branding strategy.
   e. Define risk-taking philosophy and overall risk budget.
   f. Identify and enact full-scale business model transformations.
   g. Craft the "optimal" mix of risk-taking and fee businesses.
2. **ECONOMIC VALUE CREATION AND RISK APPETITE**
   (CEO, Board of Directors, CFO, CRO)
   a. Identify economic performance and earnings targets.
   b. Determine risk budgets for business models and segments.
   c. Make large strategic principal investments.
3. **DYNAMIC MANAGEMENT (RESPONSIVE RECALIBRATIONS)**
   (CFO, ALCO, CRO, CIO, Treasurer)
   a. Perform dynamic rebalancing of systematic risks.
   b. Assign benchmarks and risk limits for active management.
   c. Make principal investments within diversification guidelines.
   d. Grow fee-based businesses and control expenses.
   e. Optimize capital structure.
   f. Design new products and enterprise-wide solutions.
4. **SYSTEMS, DATA, AND ANALYTICS**
   (CRO, Head of ALM, Operating Committee, CTO)
   a. Project accounting earnings across pivotal scenarios.
   b. Perform risk-management and economic capital analyses.
   c. Measure risk-based economic performance.
5. **PROCESS AND ORGANIZATIONAL ISSUES**
   (CFO, CRO, Head of ALM, Various Committees)
   a. Craft the "optimal" implementation of the strategic vision.
   b. Separate top-down versus bottom-up risk-taking decisions.
   c. Determine appropriate in-house versus external investments.
   d. Optimize risk-adjusted economic performance.
   e. Make tactical decisions (securitization, funding, hedging).
6. **PERSONNEL**
   a. Engender highly integrated multidisciplinary teams.
   b. Ensure collective expertise in advanced financial tools.
   c. Promote executives and advisors who can "connect the dots."
   d. Create proper long-term incentives (especially in risk taking).
7. **STAKEHOLDER COMMUNICATION**
   a. Articulate investment theses to equity and debt investors.
   b. Describe the philosophy of value creation.
   c. Demonstrate management skill and performance track record.

In what has become an important motif of this book, notice the emphasis on the changed role of risk management as it gets elevated to the level of top executive decision making along with business strategy, corporate finance, and investment activities. Risk management is no longer an afterthought or a passive safety-and-soundness verification after business decisions are made. Instead, it is a proactive and value-added resource, a component of strategic vision, and the very language of enterprise-wide strategic decisions. As risk taking and risk management become explicitly linked to the process of economic value creation, the executive charged with the responsibility for risk management gets an equal seat at the table, becoming an integral part of the executive management team.

The summary action plan designed to serve as a reminder and checklist for implementation of this book's ideas is presented on previous page.

Financial Darwinism and the Crisis of 2007–2008

As the book is going into publication, a financial crisis of dramatic (if not unprecedented) proportions continues to engulf the global financial system, causing massive devastation to real economies, financial institutions, and consumers around the world. Hundreds of billions of dollars in write downs, executive departures, government bailouts, bank runs, and demise of venerable financial institutions are all posing a stark contrast to the preceding tranquility, record profits, and prognostications that the Golden Age would never end. And yet, gratifyingly, this book's evolutionary thesis, conclusions, and recommendations remain fully intact and relevant. In particular, two different areas of lessons learned—(a) ingredients of financial success and failure in the dynamic new world, and (b) debates surrounding the nature of modern systemic financial crises—seem especially apropos to *Dynamic Finance* and *Financial Darwinism*.

Success and Failure of Financial Institutions

The first sentence of *Anna Karenina*, one of Tolstoy's best-known novels, famously observes that while "all happy families are alike; each unhappy family is unhappy in its own way." And yet when it comes to "unhappy" financial institutions that suffered losses, assorted problems, or outright ruin over the past decade, most of them were, in essence, Darwinian failures that had a great deal in common. Executives at these institutions lacked strategic vision and did not understand the changed financial landscape. Some of these executives were confused about the nature of their firm's business models altogether—for instance, failing to realize that unhedged "originate, securitize, and sell" operations were fee-based businesses only while securitization markets were functioning. These institutions lacked adequate risk management capabilities and processes. Many of them—unwilling to evolve

133

or incapable of evolving—clung to static business models, progressively de-
scending into the "bloody red oceans"[1] of commoditized businesses with
compressing margins. Eventually, this resulted in greater leverage, misunderstood risks, and inevitable sad endings.

What else distinguished some of these troubled firms? Their management succumbed to the pressures of delivering stable and growing accounting earnings, putting economic reality second and thus making noneconomic decisions. Other examples in this "unhappy" category included attempts to evolve that were not accompanied by requisite capabilities and
personnel, showing once again that dynamic risk taking is an entirely different ballgame than the task of running a traditional buy-and-hold financial
business.

On the other end of the spectrum were the firms that have successfully
weathered the pressures and financial storms. Interestingly, they too shared
common traits and behaviors, acting in the general spirit of this book's ideas
even in the absence of a unified framework. These institutions adopted an
increasingly dynamic approach to capital allocation and risk management.
They properly integrated customer-based and risk-taking decisions. Their
executives exhibited a strategic vision that was proactively communicated
to the capital markets. Their management teams collectively developed a
broad perspective and multidisciplinary expertise demanded by the complexity of today's financial businesses. They avoided asset bubbles in the
making thanks to sophisticated risk-management systems and investment
processes. These institutions based their strategic decisions on economic
considerations, refusing to cater to short-sighted perspectives of equity analysts and credit-rating agencies that rule the world of quarterly accounting
earnings reports.

The three overarching concepts in this book—*Dynamic Finance*, risk-
based economic performance, and *Financial Darwinism*—help explain the
determinants of success and failure of modern financial institutions, offering
a roadmap for their evolution in the dynamic new world.

Systemic Financial Crises

It is widely feared that the backlash to the 2007–2008 financial crisis may
involve assorted attempts to control financial globalization and "tame" capital market innovation around the world. While these endeavors are, in my
opinion, unlikely to succeed, it is virtually certain that in the coming years
we are likely to witness a wide-ranging debate on the role of public policy,
regulation, and risk management in the context of systemic financial crises.

To illustrate the impact of complex financial products on the depth
and magnitude of recent market dislocations, some financial experts have

used the following analogy. After sport utility vehicles were introduced some years ago, it was generally expected that fatality rates in car accidents would decrease due to the vehicles' improved safety features. Unfortunately, this expectation failed to materialize for a variety of reasons, including the fact that more powerful cars and better roads allowed motorists to drive faster, with more accidents occurring at higher speeds. I have always found this anecdote interesting, particularly because of its implications to regulation and risk management of financial markets. If it is in human nature to drive faster the moment better equipment (e.g., structured products or derivatives) is available, then perhaps the way to reduce death rates is to put more radar-equipped policemen (e.g., risk management) on the roads and to set appropriate speed limits (e.g., via regulation). Does this not remind you of the old-regime mental paradigm described in Chapter 2, where risk management was always a policing function and an afterthought, brought after business decisions (the speed at which to drive) were already made?

When I recently described this train of thought and its seeming conclusions to a prominent European diplomat and public policy scholar, his response was rather unexpected. He cited a different set of statistics, showing that Germany went from having much higher car accident death rates per capita relative to the United States to having much lower death rates relative to the United States over the past half century—while having much higher speed limits throughout. His observation was that it was *education*—not speed limits—that was largely responsible for this inverse development, where accident and fatality rates decreased in Germany and increased in the United States.[2] I found his argument fascinating and very relevant to the dilemmas about the role of regulation and risk management in relation to modern systemic financial crises.

Via the evolutionary perspective afforded by *Dynamic Finance,* I have argued that pressures facing static business models have gradually increased over the past quarter century. Some of these pressures (balance sheet arbitrage and fees) were secular in nature. Some (lower risk premia) were due to period-specific and cyclical factors, with an additional impact of secular forces possible. Not surprisingly, I have concluded that pressures on financial businesses become especially pronounced when the impact of all three sets of forces happens to coincide, as it indeed happened between 2003 and 2006. Which brings us back to the car accident analogy: What if motorists are being *forced* to drive faster by a combination of *external forces* and *improper incentives* during certain time periods? Then the correct response is probably not more police and lower speed limits—they are unlikely to have a desired impact en masse—but rather driver education. Motorists need to understand the global forces that make them drive faster. They need to thoroughly examine their options, alternate routes, emergency brakes, and first aid kits before they get on the road. Finally, they must be made aware of the especially dangerous environments when everyone around them is likely to drive faster as well, which may warrant a *blue ocean strategy*—taking a plane or a train to their destination instead.

How is this educational aspect relevant to the tasks of managing, understanding, and regulating financial institutions? The concept of risk-based economic performance allows us to systematically analyze the impact of external factors on the process of economic value creation. Thus, it helps detect financial crises in the making—particularly when the impacts of secular, period-specific, and cyclical forces coincide, compressing risk premia and leading to vicious circles of leverage and risk taking. In this regard, approaches proposed in this book can serve as both an educational tool and an early warning system with respect to systemic financial crises.

■ ■ ■

Despite the complexities and uncertainties that lie ahead, the forces of globalization, advances in financial theory and technology, wealth of practical experience, and best practices in risk management afford us a unique opportunity to better understand the global financial system, use the power of financial markets for the greater good, and adapt to the dynamic new world in which we find ourselves. Having spent a fair amount of time thinking about financial evolution, I now more than ever subscribe to Yogi Berra's ultimate evolutionary thesis: "The future ain't what it used to be." I do believe, however, that Darwinian success should be increasingly determined by financial institutions' dynamism as well as their willingness and ability to respond decisively to new challenges and evolve. On that note, as a final thought, I end with the passage from Norman Mailer's *The Deer Park* that powerfully summarizes this book's message:

"[T]here was that law of life so cruel and so just which demanded that one must grow or else pay more for remaining the same."

The Risk-Based Economic Performance Equation

The process of economic value creation during the static old regime was described in Chapter 2 via the following economic performance equation:

$$EP = R_A - R_L + F - E - C_C$$

where R_A and R_L are total economic returns on assets and liabilities; F and E are fees and expenses; and C_C is the cost of the firm's capital—all presented in consistent terms (percent of assets). Let us now rewrite this equation in self-explanatory dollar terms:

$$EP = \frac{\$R_A - \$R_L + \$F - \$E - \$C_C}{A}$$

or equivalently:

$$EP = \frac{A \cdot r_A - L \cdot r_L + \$F - \$E - C \cdot r_C}{A}$$

where r_A, r_L, and r_C are *rates of return* on assets, liabilities, and capital, respectively, A and L are market values of assets and liabilities, respectively, and C is the shareholders' equity equal to the difference between assets and liabilities.

Let us express rates of returns corresponding to assets and liabilities via the following market-model-type decompositions that use factors from Arbitrage Pricing Theory:

$$r_A = r_f + a_A + \sum b_{A;i} \cdot (r_{F;i} - r_f) + \varepsilon_A$$

$$r_L = r_f + a_L + \sum b_{L;i} \cdot (r_{F;i} - r_f) + \varepsilon_L$$

In the previous equations, r_f is a risk-free rate, a's are expected market-neutral excess returns, b's are factor loadings corresponding to *systematic* risk factors, $(r_{F;i} - r_f)$ are risk premia associated with systematic risk factors, and ε's are random errors that are uncorrelated with other terms.

In a deliberately less-detailed fashion, let us separate the rate of return (r_C) corresponding to the cost of capital into the risk-free rate (r_f) and excess return $(r_{C;EX})$ components as follows:

$$r_C = r_f + r_{C;EX}$$

Of course, we could have further decomposed the cost of capital into systematic and idiosyncratic risks in the previous formula, similar to what we have done with assets and liabilities. However, since the sole purpose of this decomposition is to illustrate that risk-free rates cancel out of the economic performance equation, a simpler expression sufficed. My choice was also designed to draw attention to the current practices, where the tasks of managing systematic risks vis-à-vis optimizing the weighted average cost of the capital structure are often separated and performed by different departments within financial institutions. Needless to say, capital structure optimizations may and often do affect the enterprise-wide systematic risk exposures. Hence, risk management and capital management must go hand-in-hand, which is the setting where a fuller decomposition of the rate of return on capital may become useful.

In order to glimpse into the updated economic performance equation, let us write the market-based (unrelated to fees and expenses) portion of economic performance as follows:

$$R_A - R_L - C_C = \frac{1}{A}(A \cdot r_A - L \cdot r_L - C \cdot r_C)$$

$$= r_f + a_A + \sum b_{A;i} \cdot (r_{F;i} - r_f) + \varepsilon_A - \frac{L}{A}\left(r_f + a_L + \sum b_{L;i} \cdot (r_{F;i} - r_f) + \varepsilon_L\right)$$

$$-\frac{C}{A} \cdot (r_f + r_{C;EX}) = \text{(as } r_f \text{ terms cancel out because A} = \text{L} + \text{C)}$$

$$= (a_A + \varepsilon_A) - \frac{L}{A} \cdot (a_L + \varepsilon_L) + \sum \left(b_{A;i} - \frac{L}{A} \cdot b_{L;i}\right) \cdot (r_{F;i} - r_f) - \frac{C}{A} \cdot r_{C;EX}$$

Applying these new representations of assets, liabilities, and the cost of capital to the economic performance equation, yields:

$$EP = (a_A + \varepsilon_A) - \frac{L}{A} \cdot (a_L + \varepsilon_L) + \sum \left(b_{A;i} - \frac{L}{A} \cdot b_{L;i}\right) \cdot (r_{F;i} - r_f)$$

$$+ F - E - \frac{C}{A} \cdot r_{C;EX}$$

Finally, combining expected market-neutral returns (a's) with the corresponding random errors (ε's) to arrive at market-neutral returns $\alpha_A = a_A + \varepsilon_A$ and $\alpha_L = a_L + \varepsilon_L$ (random variables), we end up with the following expression for economic performance:

$$EP = \alpha_A - \frac{L}{A}\alpha_L + \sum \left(b_{A;i} - \frac{L}{A} \cdot b_{L;i} \right) \cdot (r_{F;i} - r_f) + F - E - \frac{C}{A} r_{C;EX}$$

where α's are market-neutral excess returns for assets and liabilities.

After switching the order of terms corresponding to α_A and α_L and adopting the following notations:

$$\alpha_{ARB} = -\frac{L}{A} a_L$$
$$\alpha_{PI} = a_A$$
$$\beta_i = b_{A;i} - \frac{L}{A} b_{L;i}$$
$$RP_i = r_{F;i} - r_f$$
$$C_C = \frac{C}{A} r_{C;EX}$$

we arrive at the *Risk-Based Economic Performance Equation:*

$$EP = \alpha_{Arb} + \alpha_{PI} + \sum \beta_i \cdot RP_i + F - E - C_C$$

A Case Study in Dynamic Finance

In this section, I use the balance sheet of a hypothetical financial institution to provide some intuition behind the main concepts and themes of this book. As a disclaimer, note that this example is intended solely for illustrative purposes: to demonstrate how risk-based economic performance can be computed and linked to traditional balance sheet analyses, accounting earnings simulations, and risk management reports. While the numbers that follow are obtained via analytical and accounting analyses that were designed to be internally consistent, all results and implications—including those related to expected returns, risk measures, and the divergence of economic and accounting realities—are highly dependent of numerous subjective assumptions and financial models. All calculations are also a function of the prevailing market environment used in the analysis. I selected it to be early 2005 when, as shown in Figures 3.1 and 5.1, cyclical factors started to pressure static business models beyond the secular and period-specific forces that were already at play.

Consider the following balance sheet of a hypothetical commercial bank with $100 billion in assets and 12 percent in equity capital.

As shown in Table B.1, this institution's assets are comprised of residential mortgage-backed securities and loans, government bonds, LIBOR floaters (used, for instance, in cash management), asset-backed securities and consumer loans, commercial mortgage-backed securities and commercial real estate loans, corporate bonds and C & I loans, and municipal bonds. The liabilities, on the other hand, are comprised of certificates of deposit, other types of retail deposits, and wholesale debt that may include debentures, callable debentures, and subordinated debt instruments. For simplicity, I have assumed in this example that the institution's capital position consists exclusively of common equity. Of course, the modern view of capital may involve a variety of instruments, including hybrid capital securities, convertible bonds, and preferred stocks in addition to common equities, which has made capital structure optimization an important aspect of this book.

TABLE B.1   Hypothetical Balance Sheet

	Asset Classes	MV ($ millions)
Assets	MBS and Residential Loans	35,000
	Government Bonds	7,000
	LIBOR Floaters	20,000
	ABS and Consumer Loans	8,000
	CMBS and Comm RE Loans	9,000
	Corporate Bonds and C&I Loans	20,000
	Municipal Bonds	1,000
	Total Assets	**100,000**
Liabilities	Certificates of Deposit	5,000
	Retail of Deposit	46,000
	Wholesale Debt	37,000
	Total Liabilities	**88,000**
	Shareholder Equity	**12,000**
	Total Balance Sheet	**100,000**

Accounting Earnings and Old-Regime Economic Performance

The generation of stable and growing accounting earnings remains an over-riding objective of financial institutions at the time this book is written. Therefore, not surprisingly, considerable time and effort is spent by financial executives and their strategic advisors on modeling accounting earnings and their sensitivities to various market environments. This endeavor starts with the following calculation in Table B.2.

TABLE B.2   Margin, ROA, and ROE Calculation

	Accounting Earnings	
	$	%
Total Asset Income	5,500	5.50%
Total Liability Expense	−2,314	−2.31%
Net Interest Margin	3,186	3.19%
Non-interest Income	1,500	1.50%
Non-interest Expense	2,200	−2.20%
Loan Loss Provision	−165	−0.17%
Income (Pretax)	2,321	2.32%
Taxes	812	0.81%
ROA	1,508	1.51%
ROE	1,508	12.57%

Let us look at Table B.2 more closely. Net interest margin is, by definition, the difference between accounting returns on assets and the cost of liabilities. Loan loss provision is a heuristic adjustment for expected credit losses. Income is the net interest margin plus non-interest income minus noninterest expense minus loan loss provision. Return-on-assets (ROA) is the after-tax income presented as percentage of assets, while return-on-equity (ROE) is the after-tax income presented as percentage of shareholder equity.

In Chapter 1, I discussed the old-regime economic performance equation, stating that it represented the old way of thinking about traditional financial businesses with static business models.

$$EP = R_A - R_L + F - E - C_C$$

Not surprisingly, accounting earnings calculations in Table B.2 and various components of the old economic performance equation are closely related.

Economic Performance	Accounting Earnings Analog
$R_A - R_L$	Net Interest Margin – Loan Loss Provision
F	Non-interest Income
E	Non-interest Expense
C_C	Required ROA, RCE

Recall now the discussion in Chapter 2 on accounting earnings, business strategy, and corporate finance being the pillars of strategic decision making during the old regime. Thus, the recursive process where business decisions are formulated and accounting earnings maximized is often accompanied by the following analysis of accounting earnings and their sensitivities to changes in the market environment, shown in Table B.3.

In Table B.3, net interest margins and ROAs of the institution are simulated across a wide range of scenarios. Recession, for instance, is represented by a 100 basis point decline in interest rates (–100), a widening of credit spreads, and increase in volatilities, which is similar in spirit to Table 4.1. Other scenarios include a baseline market expectation, a recovery, a strong economic expansion where interest rates rise significantly, and extreme stress tests where interest rates increase by 300 basis points due to, say, systemic inflationary pressures. Table B.3 indicates that in the base case scenario, the institution's margins are expected to decline over time. They are also likely to be negatively affected by an increase in interest rates. While a comprehensive firm-wide picture is painted—with asset/liability returns, fees, and expenses presented side-by-side—it is not based in economic

TABLE B.3   Margin and ROA Sensitivity Analysis

	Current	Year 1	Year 2	Year 3	Year 4
Net Interest Margin					
Recession (−100)	3.05	2.83	2.74	2.72	2.65
Base Case	**3.19**	**3.14**	**3.10**	**3.11**	**3.10**
Recovery (+100)	3.09	3.34	3.37	3.43	3.53
Expansion (+200)	3.03	3.47	3.57	3.70	3.90
Stress Test (+300)	2.95	3.58	3.77	3.97	4.26
Return on Assets					
Recession (−100)	1.42	1.28	1.22	1.20	1.16
Base Case	**1.51**	**1.48**	**1.45**	**1.46**	**1.45**
Recovery (+100)	1.45	1.61	1.63	1.67	1.73
Expansion (+200)	1.41	1.69	1.76	1.84	1.97
Stress Test (+300)	1.36	1.77	1.89	2.02	2.21

reality, with fair values of assets and liabilities not calculated to properly capture the impact of potential changes in external environments.

Risk Management

Throughout the book, I have emphasized the disconnect that often existed between risk management and executive strategic decisions during the old regime. In fact, risk-taking was neither explicit nor dynamic within static business models. Tables B.2 and B.3 illustrate this point. The delivery of stable accounting earnings is a dominant objective achieved through business strategy and corporate finance. Once business decisions are made, standard management reports similar to the one shown in Table B.4 can be used to monitor the risk on an ongoing basis in order to ensure the safety and soundness of the institution. Still, describing the business model of the institution, or understanding the relative importance of risk taking vis-à-vis other drivers of economic performance, or using this report in executive-level strategic decisions remains challenging.

In Table B.4—that operates in terms of assets and liabilities just like the old economic performance equation does—various dimensions of risks and economic returns are presented side by side for different asset classes and the balance sheet as a whole. EROR (expected rate of return) is the total expected economic return over a particular horizon, say one year. This is exactly the measure used in the calculation of the $R_A - R_L$ term of the economic performance equation. Partial durations describe exposures along specific risk dimensions. Thus, OAD (option-adjusted duration) and OAC

TABLE B.4   Risk Management Analysis

	MV ($millions)	EROR (%)	Partial Durations				Key Rate Durations				Value-at-Risk (Annual, 95%)			
			OAD	OAC	MBD	VOL	3-mo	2-yr	5-yr	10-yr	System	Credit	Specific	Total
Assets														
MBS and Residential Loans	35,000	6.23%	2.7	(1.8)	2.2	(0.2)	0.1	0.7	0.5	1.3	1.75%		0.78%	1.92%
Government Bonds	7,000	5.04%	6.6	0.5			(0.0)	(0.1)	2.0	4.6	0.41%		0.00%	0.41%
LIBOR Floaters	20,000	2.45%	0.3	0.0			0.2	(0.0)	0.0	0.0	0.00%		0.14%	0.14%
ABS and Consumer Loans	8,000	5.38%	3.2	0.4	0.0		0.1	0.3	0.1	2.4	2.31%	0.63%	2.33%	3.34%
CMBS and Comm RE Loans	9,000	5.50%	1.6	0.1			0.0	0.1	1.1	0.4	0.43%	0.09%	0.00%	0.44%
Corporate Bonds and C&I Loans	20,000	5.21%	1.7	(0.0)		(0.0)	0.1	0.5	0.8	0.2	1.00%	0.16%	0.30%	1.05%
Municipal Bonds	1,000	5.38%	3.3	(0.2)	(0.1)	(0.1)	(0.2)	0.8	0.6	1.7	1.97%	0.50%	0.00%	2.03%
Total Assets	**100,000**	**5.04%**	**2.2**	**(0.4)**	**0.8**	**(0.1)**	**0.1**	**0.4**	**0.6**	**1.1**	**5.70%**	**0.17%**	**2.48%**	**6.22%**
Liabilities Certificates of Deposit	5,000	3.86%	2.3	0.1			0.1	0.8	1.2	0.0	0.47%		0.00%	0.47%
Retail Deposits	46,000	1.76%	3.6	0.3			0.1	0.3	1.2	1.8	0.37%		0.00%	0.37%
Wholesale Debt	37,000	3.80%	0.4	0.0			0.2	0.2	(1.0)	0.9	4.96%	0.25%	0.79%	5.03%
Total Liabilities	**88,000**	**2.74%**	**2.2**	**0.2**	**0.8**		**0.1**	**0.3**	**0.3**	**1.3**	**5.72%**	**0.11%**	**1.53%**	**5.92%**
Total Balance Sheet	**100,000**	**2.63%**	**0.3**	**(0.5)**	**0.8**	**(0.1)**	**0.0**	**0.1**	**0.3**	**(0.1)**	**1.57%**	**0.12%**	**2.91%**	**3.31%**

* All expected return numbers are presented as percentages of the corresponding market values.

(option-adjusted convexity) are first- and second-order sensitivities to parallel changes in interest rates. MBD (mortgage basis duration) is the sensitivity to changes in mortgage spreads. VOL (volatility duration) is the sensitivity to changes in implied volatilities. Key rate durations represent sensitivities to movements of specific regions of the yield curve (3-mo, 2-yr, 5-yr, and 10-yr). The last block is devoted to annualized Value-at-Risk measured at the 95 percent confidence level. Value-at-Risk is divided into systematic ("System") and security-specific ("Specific") components. The overall credit risk ("Credit"), a component of the "System" VaR, is shown separately since, unlike other systematic risks, credit risk is difficult to describe through such parametric risk measures as spread durations. As mentioned in Chapter 4, specific choices of risk measures are immaterial for the purposes of this book. As opposed (or in addition) to Value-at-Risk, I could have chosen coherent Value-at-Risk, economic capital, scenario analyses, or stress tests to describe the risks inherent in this hypothetical balance sheet. Definitions of these risk measures and their practical applications can be found in Golub and Tilman (2000) and other risk-management textbooks.

Table B.4 suggests that the balance sheet in our example is managed fairly conservatively. Differential systematic risks between assets and liabilities are relatively small, with only moderate sensitivity to changes in interest rates, yield curve, and implied volatilities. The majority of differential return between assets and liabilities appears to be due to mortgage basis exposure and security-specific risks. These conclusions can be used to describe the nature of the carry trade embedded in the balance sheet.

Economic versus Accounting Realities

Before we transition to the discussion of risk-based economic performance, let us briefly compare the accounting and economic realities at hand, which are displayed in Table B.5.

In Table B.5, accounting and economic returns for major line items on the income statement are presented side by side. Notice that in our example, net interest margin *adjusted for loan loss provision* does not appear dramatically different from the differential economic return between assets and liabilities, (3.19%–0.17% versus 2.63%). However, this difference is enough to deem the institution viable from the accounting earnings perspective and not viable from the economic returns perspective, as least during the time period in question. To illustrate that, let us assume that the institution's required return on equity capital is 12 percent, which can be translated into the required pretax ROA of 2.22 percent. It can be seen that

TABLE B.5   Accounting Earnings vs. Economic Returns

	Accounting Earnings		Economic Returns	
	$	%	$	%
Total Asset Income	5,500	5.50%	5,044	5.04%
Total Liability Expense	−2,314	−2.31%	−2,411	−2.41%
Net Interest Margin	3,186	3.19%	2,634	2.63%
Non-Interest Income	1,500	1.50%	1,500	1.50%
Non-Interest Expense	−2,200	−2.20%	−2,200	−2.20%
Loan Loss Provision	−165	−0.17%		
Income (Pre-tax)	2,321	2.32%	1,934	1.93%
Pre-tax ROA		2.32%		1.93%
Required Pre-tax ROA		2.22%		2.22%
EP		0.11%		−0.28%
ROE		12.57%		10.47%
Required ROE		12.00%		12.00%

All percent returns are presented as percent of assets.

while accounting-based pretax ROA is 2.32% > 2.22%, its economic analog is 1.93% < 2.22%. This can be equivalently presented in terms of economic performance, which is negative:

$$EP = R_A - R_L + F - E - C_C < 0$$
$$EP = 5.04\% - 2.41\% + 1.5\% - 2.20\% - 2.22\% = -0.28 < 0$$

Note that the difference between economic and accounting returns can be due to multiple reasons. First, the adjustment for credit risk as given by the loan loss provision may be different from credit risk models embedded in the economic rate of return calculations. Second, other cash flow uncertainties, such as short embedded options, mortgage prepayments, and credit rating migrations, are usually captured in economic return but not accounting earnings calculations. As seen from Table B.5, the view on something as fundamental as the economic viability of financial institutions may differ substantially between accounting and economic realities.

Significant divergence between economic and accounting realities may be present in the risk estimates as well. Consider the following scenario analysis, wherein the impacts of various market shocks on the institution's assets, liabilities, and equity are estimated. As seen from the risk-management numbers in Table B.4, the balance sheet is positioned fairly conservatively, with no significant mismatches between assets and liabilities present, and Value-at-Risk numbers indicative of the moderate overall risk. This is consistent with Table B.6 that shows accounting and economic sensitivities of

TABLE B.6 Accounting Risk vs. Economic Risk

		Recession Rates: −100	Base Case	Recovery Rates: +100	Expansion Rates: +200	Stress Test Rates: +300
Assets	Accounting	103,544	100,000	98,078	95,828	93,635
	Fair Value	102,232	100,000	97,772	95,548	93,328
	Difference (%)	1.28%		0.31%	0.29%	0.33%
Liabilities	Accounting	89,251	88,000	87,065	86,180	85,343
	Fair Value	89,711	88,000	86,288	84,574	82,859
	Difference (%)	−0.51%		0.90%	1.90%	3.00%
Equity	Accounting	14,293	12,000	11,013	9,648	8,292
	Fair Value	12,521	12,000	11,484	10,974	10,469
	Difference (%)	14.15%		−4.11%	−12.08%	−20.80%
Equity at Risk	Accounting	19%	0%	−8%	−20%	−31%
	Fair Value	4%	0%	−4%	−9%	−13%
	Difference (%)	339.77%		91.41%	129.19%	142.23%

assets as similar: in anticipation of a rise in interest rates and a flattening of the yield curve, assets used in our example did not have a lot of embedded options and were characterized by relatively short durations. However, notice the significant difference in accounting-based versus economic sensitivities of liabilities to changes in market environments. Due to various assumptions and conventions, accounting methods significantly underestimated the duration of liabilities in this case and, hence, they overestimated the losses across higher interest-rate scenarios. As scenarios involving assets and liabilities are translated into equity terms, discrepancies get significantly amplified by leverage, resulting in dramatically different conclusions about the sensitivity of shareholder equity to changes in market environments.

As before, it is important to emphasize the illustrative nature of Table B.6. and other results in this Appendix. Our goal here is to demonstrate that accounting and economic analyses can arrive as fairly different estimates of risks and returns—nothing more. Sometimes accounting earnings will overestimate returns and risks. Sometimes it will be the other way around, so no general conclusions can be reached. As stated throughout this book, accounting and economic realities can diverge significantly, which calls for a simultaneous optimization of both by real-world financial institutions for the foreseeable future.

Risk-Based Economic Performance and Its Attribution

So far, a combination of accounting and risk-management analyses have afforded us some important insights into the risk/return characteristics of this hypothetical financial institution, including the risks underlying the carry trade on the balance sheet. However, I would argue that the description of its process of economic value creation (i.e., risk-based business model) still remains incomplete, warranting an application of the risk-based economic performance equation:

$$EP = \alpha_{Arb} + \alpha_{PI} + \sum \beta_i \cdot RP_i + F - E - C_C$$

where, as before, α_{Arb} stands for balance sheet arbitrage; α_{PI} represents market-neutral principal investment activities; $\sum \beta_i \cdot RP_i$ denotes exposures to systematic risks; F and E stand for fees and expenses, respectively, and C_C represents the cost of capital.

Through financial modeling, differential returns between assets and liabilities can be broken into three dominant risk-based components: balance sheet arbitrage, principal investments, and systematic risks. Subsequently, economic performance and its attribution ratios can be used to intuitively

TABLE B.7   Economic Performance Attribution

	Economic Returns		
	EROR	EP	Attrib
Differential A/L Returns	2.63%		
Balance Sheet Arbitrage		1.70%	88%
Principal Investments		0.75%	39%
Systematic Risks		0.18%	10%
Fees	1.50%	1.50%	78%
Total Risk Taking and Fees		**4.13%**	214%
Expenses	−2.20%	−2.20%	−114%
EP (before capital)	1.93%	**1.93%**	100%
Cost of Capital	2.22%	2.22%	
Economic Performance		**-0.28%**	

describe the portfolio of business models of a financial institution in greater detail than via the old-fashioned economic performance equation.

According to Table B.7, the majority of economic performance of this institution comes from balance sheet arbitrage and fee-based activities, with principal investments and systematic risks playing significant yet secondary roles. The overall risk-based business model is described via economic performance attribution ratios ("Attrib"). Thus, for instance, the contribution of balance sheet arbitrage is as defined in Chapter 3:

$$EPA_{ARB} = \frac{\alpha_{Arb}}{\alpha_{Arb} + \alpha_{PI} + \sum \beta_i \cdot RP_i + F - E} = 88\%$$

Transparency and Equity Valuation Implications

Economic performance attribution presents all economic earnings drivers in a consistent fashion, affording intuitive descriptions of business models and risk/return profiles of financial institutions. As a result, differences in business models across institutions can be illuminated as well. For instance, the risk inherent in an institution that generates the vast majority of economic performance through balance sheet arbitrage should be substantially less than that of a firm that creates the majority of economic value through principal investment activities. In Chapter 5, I postulated that as financial institutions move toward risk-based disclosures and fair valuation, economic performance attribution ratios are also likely to become more directly linked to equity market valuations. Let us illustrate the links between economic performance and equity market valuations in Table B.8 as follows.

TABLE B.8   Economic Performance Attribution and Equity Valuation

	Economic Returns						Accounting Earnings	
	Institution #1				Institution #2		Institutions 1 and 2	
	EROR	EP	Attrib	Mult	Attrib	Mult	%	Mult
Total Asset Income	5.04%						5.50%	
Total Liability Expense	−2.41%						−2.31%	
Net Interest Margin	2.63%						3.19%	14
Balance Sheet								
Arbitrage		1.70%	**88%**	20	**51%**	20		
Principal Investments		0.75%	**39%**	10	**61%**	10		
Systematic Risks		0.18%	**10%**	12	**24%**	12		
Non-interest Income	1.50%	1.50%	**78%**	20	**78%**	20	1.50%	20
Non-interest Expense	−2.20%	−2.20%	**−114%**	20	**−114%**	20	−2.20%	20
Total	1.93%	1.93%	100%	**15**	100%	**12**		**12**

As shown in Table B.8, the financial institution in our example delivers the majority of differential asset/liability returns through balance sheet arbitrage, with principal investments and systematic risks playing secondary roles. Meanwhile, imagine a competitor ("Institution #2) that generates a significantly larger percentage of economic performance through principal investments and systematic risks. Let us assume that the two institutions have exactly the same contributions of fees and expenses to economic performance.

As argued in Chapter 5 and related to Figure 5.6, the difference in business models between the two institutions may not be visible to external stakeholders due to the lack of risk-based disclosures. From the viewpoint of accounting earnings, the two institutions are identical: Their differential asset/liability returns presented as summary numbers are the same, and, therefore, capital markets are likely to assign same P/E ratios to both. Thus, a typical commercial banking A/L business may get a P/E ratio of 14, while fee-based businesses and expenses may receive a P/E ratio of 20. Both institutions, therefore, may receive a P/E ratio of 12 despite very different business models shown through economic performance attribution. A greater differentiation would likely occur if the information about the institutions' economic performance attribution were available, as shown in Table B.8. While Institution #2 in fact deserves the multiple of 12, Institution #1 should be valued at 15 (weighted average multiple based on economic performance attribution ratios) due to the superior risk-based business model mix. For Institution #1 to achieve premium equity market valuation, components of economic performance need to be measured and communicated to external stakeholders in a proactive fashion.

It is noteworthy that economic performance attribution has applications beyond strategic management and equity market analysis. This methodology can be employed in risk-focused regulation by helping distinguish between different business models of similarly chartered institutions.

Dynamic Management and Responsive Recalibrations of Business Models

Let us now switch gears and discuss the management and organizational aspects of this example. Recall that the market environment used in this analysis was early 2005, when financial market expectations were pointing toward a sustainable expansion both in the United States and globally. This is precisely how our financial institution appears to be positioned. Interest rate risk of the balance sheet is minimal, which should bode well in a rising rate and flattening yield curve environment. Exposure to mortgage prepayments is significant, which again is consistent with the expectation for slower mortgage prepayments. However, exposures to implied volatilities and credit risk are rather small; one would expect them to be playing a larger role on the balance sheet during an expansion.

The precision with which systematic risks of the institution are aligned with the macroeconomic view is unlikely to be accidental. One possible explanation is that the executive management of the firm is engaged in responsive recalibrations of the business model, particularly as far as systematic risks are concerned. In an analog of Figure 4.2, the transition from a recessionary positioning to the current one could have occurred via the following ALCO process described in Figure B.1.

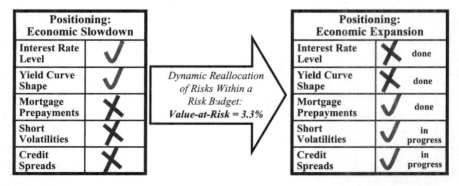

FIGURE B.1 Current Positioning as a Result Dynamic Management of Systematic Risks

While interest rate, yield curve shape, and mortgage prepayment dimensions are already recalibrated, adjustments of volatility and credit dimensions appear in progress.

This dynamic recalibration of systematic risks could have been achieved through a variety of advanced financial tools from Figure 4.6. Thus, the reduction in duration could have been implemented through asset strategies, securitization, debt restructuring, or derivatives hedging, as shown in Figure B.2.

The dynamic rebalancing of systematic risks depicted in Figure B.1 would have worked well in 2005 and early 2006. However, exposures to mortgage spreads, credit, and volatilities should have been reduced in mid to late 2006, with interest rate and yield curve exposures increasing accordingly: By that time, the leverage in the system was approaching especially dangerous levels and the housing market deterioration became likely, sparking the 2007–2008 credit and liquidity crisis shortly thereafter.

Risk-Based Business Model and Executive Decisions

In our example, the risk-based business model of this institution could have been a result of the top-down decision-making process described in Chapter 4. As shown in Figure B.3, the risk/return characteristics of the business model first determined on a macrolevel, followed by an increasingly specific

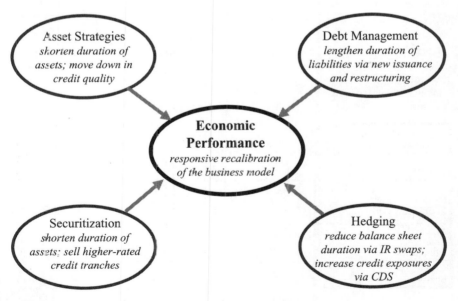

FIGURE B.2 Universe of Financial Tools Used to Rebalance Systematic Risks

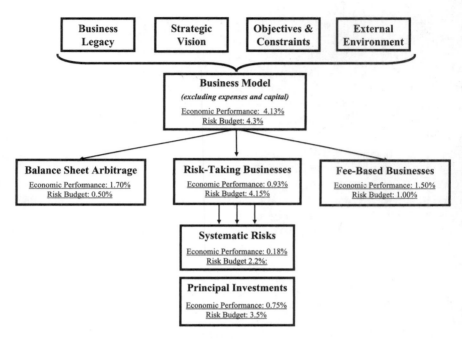

FIGURE B.3 Executive-Level Strategic Decision-Making Tree

TABLE B.9   Risk-Based Business Model Report

	Economic Returns			VaR (M&C)	VaR (Other)	VaR Total
	EROR	EP	Attrib			
Differential A/L Returns	2.63%			3.3%		3.3%
Balance Sheet Arbitrage		1.70%	88%		0.5%	0.5%
Principal Investments		0.75%	39%	2.9%	2.0%	3.5%
Systematic Risks		0.18%	10%	1.6%	1.5%	2.2%
Fees	1.50%	1.50%	78%		1.0%	1.0%
Total Risk Taking and Fees		4.13%	214%	3.3%	2.7%	4.3%
Expenses	−2.20%	−2.20%	−114%			
EP (before capital)	1.93%	1.93%	100%	3.3%	2.7%	4.3%
Cost of Capital	2.22%	2.22%				
Economic Performance		−0.28%				4.3%

Note: "M&C" stands for market and credit risk.
"Other" encompasses liquidity, funding, operational, and other risks.

identification of the role of various fee-based and risk-taking activities in the delivery of economic performance.

In place of disparate accounting earnings and risk reports depicting different aspects of the institution's balance sheet and business model, the risk-based business model report in Table B.9 provides a concise description of the earnings drivers and inherent risks. As discussed in Chapter 4, once strategic executive decisions are made, economic performance attribution and risk analyses can be used to explicitly optimize risk-adjusted economic performance.

Strategic management of real-world financial institutions is a complex and multifaceted endeavor that spans business strategy, corporate finance, risk management, and investment decisions. In this example, I tried to numerically illustrate some of this book's main themes and concepts, including:

- risk-based business models and economic performance
- pillars of strategic decision making
- executive-level strategic vision and its implementation
- dynamic risk-taking decisions and business model transformations
- coexistance and potential divergence of accounting and economic realities
- linkages between business models, transparency, and equity market valuations.

Notes

Preface

1. See Druker (2004).
2. See Kim and Mauborgne (2005).
3. See Friedman (2007).
4. I borrow the term *filtering out complexity* from James Wilk's forthcoming book *Rethinking Reality*.

Chapter 1

1. These quotes belong to (a) Harvard Management's CEO Mohamed El-Erian (see B. Alpert, "Bringing Analysis to Bear and Bull," *Barron's*, June 18, 2007) ; (b) Goldman Sachs CEO Lloyd Blankfein (see "High State of Nervousness," *Wall Street Journal*, June 27 2007); and (c) Richard Bove, an analyst with Punk, Ziegel & Co. (see J. Creswell, "A New Genre on Wall St," *The New York Times*. June 28 2007) and Chairman of FDIC.
2. See Ferguson and Oliver Wyman, *The Evolution of Financial Services* (2007).
3. For a discussion on the flow of risks and an updated perspective on financial intermediation, see Ho, Lee, and Tilman's *The Risk Paradigm*.
4. See Rappaport (1997).
5. See Ferguson and Wyman, *The Evolution of Financial Services* (2007).
6. See Bernanke (2004) and Blanchard and Simon (2001). It was documented that the variability of quarterly growth in real output, as measured by its standard deviation, has declined by half since the mid-1980s, while the variability of quarterly inflation has declined by about two thirds.
7. See Borio (2007), page 1.
8. See Bernanke, (2005).
9. Source: Ryan ALM, Inc., 2008.
10. See Golub and Tilman (2000).

11. I borrow this phrase from the proceedings of the 2007 Annual Meeting of the World Economic Forum in Davos.
12. I owe the term *responsive recalibrations* to Francesco Ceccato.
13. For details and references in this section see Chapter 5.

Chapter 2

1. See Copeland and Weston (1988).
2. EVA was introduced by Stern Stewart & Co. and described in Young and O'Byrne (2000). While EVA is an after-tax metric, economic performance calculation can be done either in pretax or after-tax terms: Either returns, fees, and expenses can be presented on the posttax basis, or alternatively the cost of capital can be presented on the pretax basis, as illustrated in Appendix B.
3. This can be seen, for instance, from the properties of equity valuation models that operate in terms of price-to-earnings ratios, as discussed in Sharpe, Alexander, and Bailey (1999) or Ross, Westerfield, and Jordan (2007). Thus, zero economic performance can be thought of as analogous to the zero-growth dividend model, where the P–E ratio of a fairly priced stock is likely to remain unchanged over time under normal circumstances. On the other hand, as can be seen most easily from the constant growth models, persistently negative economic performance is likely to result in declining P–E ratios if all other factors remain fixed.
4. Financial services' statistics are from Ferguson and Oliver Wyman (2007).
5. See "Securitization in Latin America," *BIS Quarterly Review*, September 2007, and "Milken Says Credit Could Free $100 Trillion for Poor," *Bloomberg News*, Jan 18, 2007.
6. As an interesting side note on disintermediation, the 2007 credit and liquidity crisis saw a temporary resurrection of traditional intermediation patterns; for example, the majority of mortgage issuance returned to being largely performed by commercial banks as securitization outlets became unavailable.
7. See Sharpe et al. (1999) and Brown (2007), respectively.
8. See Mishkin (2005).
9. See K. French, "The Cost of Active Investing," Working Paper, March (2008).
10. Source: Highline Financial and National Credit Union Administration. For the credit union industry as a whole, weighted average ROAA of 0.96 percent in 2001 declined to 0.74 percent in 2007. For more details on business models of credit unions, see a case study in Ho, Lee, and Tilman (2009).

11. See Moody's Life Insurance Industry Outlook, January 2004.
12. I owe this metaphor to Wade Barnett.
13. See "A sudden squall upsets investors' structured thinking" by Gillian Tett, *Financial Times*, June 16–17 2007.
14. See *New York Times*, December 3, 2007, Krugman, Paul, "Innovating Our Way to Financial Crisis," Op-Ed.

Chapter 3

1. As a representative case in point, Jeremy Grantham, GMO's Chairman of the Board, has been quoted as saying that hedge funds have adopted a practice of "piling on risk of different kinds and presenting it as outperformance" (http://www.seekingalpha.com/article/43242-jeremy-grantham-hedge-funds-to-collapse).
2. I borrow these representations from the market model and the Arbitrage Pricing Theory (see Sharpe and Alexander (1998) and Ross (1976), respectively).
3. See Tilman (2003).
4. Alternative approaches to modeling bank deposits and subjective assumptions may significantly affect the estimates of both interest rate and yield curve exposures of bank balance sheets.
5. In this discussion, I follow the market convention of using LIBOR as a benchmark for both GSE debt issuance as well as investments involving mortgage-backed securities and loans. Other benchmarks (e.g., AAA-rated financial yield curves) could be used in this exercise as well.

Chapter 4

1. See Ho, Lee, and Tilman (2009).
2. See Ibbotson and Kaplan (2000).
3. See Fabozzi (2005), Ed., *The Handbook of Mortgage-Backed Securities* (6th ed.), McGraw-Hill.
4. *Economic capital* is defined as the amount of capital that is needed to ensure that a financial institution remains solvent over a certain time period and with a given confidence level (see Porteous and Tapadar, 2005). For descriptions of other modern risk measures, see Golub and Tilman (2000).
5. Incorporation of factors that are currently defined as *noneconomic* into the decision-making process and optimizations frameworks may also be possible, which makes this discussion relevant for double- and triple-bottom-line companies.

6. See Nassim Taleb's *The Black Swan: The Impact of the Highly Improbable* and Michael Raynor's *The Strategy Paradox: Why Committing to Success Leads to Failure.*

7. I borrow these expressions from James Wilk's upcoming book *Rethinking Reality.*

Chapter 5

1. See Goldman Sachs (2006) annual report.

2. Balance Sheet Arbitrage: Wachovia presentation at Lehman Brothers Financial Services Conference (September 10, 2007) and the case study on the Farm Credit System in Ho, Lee, Tilman (2009), and Fannie Mae and Freddie Mac's chapters in L. Tilman's *Asset/Liability Management of Financial Institutions.* Principal Investments: *Financial Times* and *WSJ.* Systematic Risks: PIMCO's Investment Commentaries by William Gross, CIO. Fees: *WSJ* and Bloomberg. Expenses: *New York Times* and *WSJ.* Capital Structure: Accelerated Share Repurchases: Excess Market Returns, and Accelerated Share Repurchases, Bear Stearns, September 13, 2007 and April 3, 2007 and http://pwc.blogs.com/mohammed_amin/2006/02/hybrid_capital_.html.

3. Sources are as follows. Transition away from static business models via greater allocations to alternative investments: *WSJ*, Infovest21 News Provider Service, *WSJ* MarketBeat blog, *Financial Times*, *AFP*, Institutional Investor and Bloomberg. Transition away from static business models via dynamic management of systematic risks: Company's releases, *WSJ*, and Bloomberg. Transformation of risk-taking into fee-based business via securitization: Company press releases, 247wallst.com. Integration of strategic advice, financing, and principal investment activities: *WSJ* and Bloomberg citing the 10/30/07 letter of Goldman Sachs' Chief Accounting Officer Sarah Smith to the Securities and Exchange Commission that was made public. On a related matter, see the case study of investment banks business models in Ho, Lee, and Tilman (2009). Shorting options via acquisitions of reinsurance companies and other means: Company reports and SNL Financial Coupling of fee-based services: Company releases, HBR.

4. Y. Onaran, "Wall Street Gets Lift from SEC Rule, May Earn $4.4 Billion More," *Bloomberg News,* June 10, 2007.

5. See the discussion on investment banks' business models in Ho, Lee, and Tilman (2009).

6. Some of approaches relevant to this task can be found in Lo (2007).

7. Sources: Company filings, Bloomberg LP, IDG News Service.

8. I owe some of the insights regarding the applicability of *Dynamic Finance* to nonfinancial corporations and related institutional examples to Wolfgang Kessler, CEO of FireApps, Inc., and Andy Gage, Vice President of FireApps, Inc.

9. See *Financial Times*, Nov 13, 2007.

10. Various activities of modern financial institutions and institutional investors—ranging from risk management to valuation to balance sheet management—rely on numerous assumptions and uncertainties inherent in financial models and analytical systems. For instance, mortgage valuation models rely on econometric estimates of prepayments as well as on stochastic processes according to which interest rates and other market factors are expected to evolve. Model risks refer to potential losses that may be incurred if assumptions and estimates underlying analytical models turn out to be incorrect.

11. See Borio (2007), page 2.

12. See Borio (2005), page 10.

13. See "The summer bloodbath: Not a quant problem; just a problem," Ft.com, September 25 2007.

14. Part of this discussion is based on Golub and Tilman (2000). Also, I owe some of the insights regarding complexity and diffusion of risks in 2007–2008 to Bennett Golub.

15. See "Governments are urged to make lenders bear some risk on securitized loans," *WSJ*, Nov 13, 2007.

16. This is discussed at length in Ho, Lee, and Tilman's *The Risk Paradigm*.

17. See "Goldman Sachs profits in credit crisis after slicing its mortgage risk," *New York Times*, December 2007.

Epilogue

1. See Kim and Mauborgne (2005).

2. I owe this insight to Dr. Klaus Scharioth, the Ambassador of the Federal Republic of Germany to the United States.

Appendix A

1. See Sharpe et al. (1998) and Ross (1976).

References

Arnott, Robert D., and Peter L. Bernstein. "What Risk Premium 'Is Normal'?" *Financial Analysts Journal* 58, 2 (2002), 64–85.

Beinhocker, E., *Origin of Wealth: Evolution, Complexity, and the Radical Remaking of Economics*. Boston: Harvard Business School Press, 2007.

Blanchard, Olivier, and John Simor. (2001). "The Long and Large Decline in U.S. Output Volatility. *Brookings Papers on Economic Activity* 1 (2001), 135–64.

Bernanke, B. *Regulation and Financial Innovation*. Presentation at the Federal Reserve Bank of Atlanta's 2007 Financial Markets Conference, May 15, 2007.

Bernanke, B. *The Global Saving Glut and the U.S. Current Account Deficit*. FRB: The Homer Jones Lecture, St. Louis, Missouri, April 2005.

Bernanke, B., Thomas Laubach, Frederic S. Mishkin, & Adam S. Posen, *Inflation Targeting: Lessons from the International Experience*. Princeton: Princeton University Press, 2001.

Bernanke, B. *The Great Moderation*. Remarks at the meetings of the Eastern Economic Association, Washington, DC, February 20, 2004.

Bernstein, P. *Against the Gods: The Remarkable Story of Risk*. New York: John Wiley & Sons, 1998.

Borio, C. *Change and Constancy in the Financial System: Implications for the Financial Distress and Policy*. Bank for International Settlements Working Paper, August, 2007.

Brown, J. *Financial Deregulation: The Need for Safeguards*. GIS Action Project for Economic and Social Justice, 2007.

Carret, P. *The Art of Speculation*. New York: John Wiley & Sons, 1997.

Copeland T., and J. F. Weston. *Financial Theory and Corporate Policy*, (3rd ed). Reading, MA: Addison-Wesley, 1988.

Davenport, T., and J. Harris. *Competing on Analytics: The New Science of Winning*. Boston: Harvard Business School Press, 2007.

Drucker, P. *The Daily Drucker: 366 Days of Insight and Motivation for Getting the Right Things Done*. New York: Collins, 2004.

Duffie, D., and K. Singleton. *Credit Risk: Pricing, Measurement, and Management*. Princeton: Princeton University Press, 2003.

Elton, E., M. Gruber, S. Brown, and W. Goetzmann, *Modern Portfolio Theory and Investment Analysis*. Hoboken, NJ: John Wiley & Sons, 2003.

Ferguson, Niall, and Oliver Wyman. *The Evolution of Financial Services*. New York: Oliver Wyman, 2007.

Friedman, B. *The Moral Consequences of Economic Growth*. New York: Vintage Books, 2005.

Friedman, T. *The World is Flat: A Brief History of the Twenty-first Century*. New York: Picador, 2007.

Gilles C., L. Rubin, J. Ryding, L. Tilman, and A. Rajadhyaksha. Long-term economic and market trends and their implications for asset/liability management of insurance companies. *Journal of Risk Finance*, Winter 2003.

Goetzmann, W., and R. Ibbotson. *The Equity Risk Premium: Essays and Explorations*. New York: Oxford University Press, 2006.

Golub, Tilman. *Risk Management: Approaches for Fixed Income Markets*. New York: John Wiley & Sons, 2000.

Greenspan, A. *Reflections on central banking*. Proceedings of the "The Greenspan Era: Lessons for the Future" Symposium Sponsored by the Federal Reserve Bank of Kansas City, Jackson Hole, WY, August 25–27, 2005.

Grinold R., and R. Kahn, *Active Portfolio Management: A Quantitative Approach to Producing Superior Returns and Controlling Risk* (2nd ed.). New York: McGraw-Hill, 2000.

Gulati, R. "Silo Busting: How to Execute on the Promise of Customer Focus." *Harvard Business Review* (May 1, 2007): 98–108.

Hammer, M. and J. Champy, *Reengineering the Corporation: A Manifesto for Business Revolution*. New York: Collins, 2006.

Ho, T. S. Y., S. B. Lee, and L. M. Tilman. *The Risk Paradigm: Understanding Modern Financial Institutions and Business Models*. New York: Oxford University Press, forthcoming 2009.

Ibbotson, R., and P. Kaplan, "Does Asset Allocation Policy Explain 40, 90, and 100 percent of Performance?" *Financial Analysts Journal* (January/February 2000): 26–33.

Johnson, Spencer. *Who Moved my Cheese: An Amazing Way to Deal with Change in Your Work and in Your Life*. New York: G. P. Putnam's Sons, 1998.

Kim, W.C., and R. Mauborgne, *Blue Ocean Strategy: How to Create Uncontested Market Space and Make Competition Irrelevant*, Boston: Harvard Business School Press, 2005.

Kindlerberger, C. *Manias, Panics, and Crashes: A History of Financial Crises*. New York: John Wiley & Sons, 1996.

Litterman, R. *Modern Investment Management: An Equilibrium Approach*. Hoboken, NJ: John Wiley & Sons, 2003.

Lo, A. "Where Do Alphas Come From: A New Measure of Value of Active Investment Management." MIT Working Paper, 2007.

Lowenstein, R. *When Genius Failed: The Rise and Fall of Long-Term Capital Management*. New York: Random House, 2000.

Makay, C., and J. De La Vega, *Extraordinary Popular Delusions and the Madness of the Crowds and Confusion de Confusiones*. New York: John Wiley & Sons, 1996.

Malkiel, B. *A Random Walk Down Wall Street*. New York: Norton, 1999.

Mankiw, G. *Macroeconomics* (5th ed). New York: Worth, 2003.

Merton, R. *Future Possibilities in Finance Theory and Practice*. Keynote Address at the World Congress of the Bachelier Finance Society, June, 2000.

Mishkin, F. S, and S. G. Eakins, *Financial Markets and Institutions*. Upper Saddle River, NJ: Addison Wesley, 2005.

Moody's Life Insurance Industry Outlook, January (2004).

Pagano, M., "How Theories of Financial Intermediation and Corporate Risk-management Influence Bank Risk-taking Behavior." *Financial Markets, Institutions & Instruments* 10 (5) (2001): 203–323.

Porteous, Bruce T., & Pradip Tapadar. *Economic Capital and Financial Risk Management for Financial Services Firms and Conglomerates*. New York: Palgrave Macmillan, 2005.

Rappaport, A. *Creating Shareholder Value: A Guide for Managers and Investors*. New York: Free Press, 1997.

Raynor, M. *The Strategy Paradox: Why Committing to Success Leads to Failure*. New York: Currency Doubleday, 2007.

Ross, S. "The Arbitrage Theory of Capital Asset Pricing." *Journal of Economic Theory*, 13 (3) (1976): 341–360.

Ross S., R., Westerfield, and B. Jordan. *Fundamentals of Corporate Finance*, 8th ed. New York: McGraw-Hill/Irwin, 2007.

Rubinstein, M. "Great Moments in Financial Economics: Modigliani-Miller Theorem." *Journal of Investment Management*, Q2 (2003).

Sharpe, W., G. J. Alexander, and J. W. Bailey. *Investments* (6th ed). Upper Saddle River, NJ: Prentice Hall, 1998.

Siegel, Jeremy J. "The Shrinking Equity Premium." *Journal of Portfolio Management, Fall*, 26 (1): 10–17.

Taleb, N. *Black Swan: The Impact of the Highly Improbable*. New York: Random House, 2007.

Taleb, N., *Fooled by Randomness* (2nd ed). New York: Random House, 2005.

Tilman, L. (Ed.) *Asset/Liability Management of Financial Institutions: Maximizing Shareholder Value through Risk-Conscious Investing*. Euromoney Institutional Investor, 2003.

United States Government Accountability Office. *State and Local Government Retirement Benefits: Current Status of Benefit Structures, Protections, and Fiscal Outlook for Funding Costs.* Report to the Committee on Finance, U.S. Senate. Washington, September 2007. (GAO-07-1156).

Van Deventer, D., K. Imai, and M. Mesler. *Advanced Financial Risk Management: Tools and Techniques for Integrated Credit Risk and Interest Rate Risk Management.* Hoboken, NJ: John Wiley & Sons 2005.

Warnock, F., and V. Warnock "International Capital Flows and U.S. Interest Rates." Board of Governors of the Federal Reserve System, International Finance Discussion Papers, No. 840, September, 2005.

Wilmott, Paul. *Paul Wilmott on Quantitative Finance* (2nd ed). Hoboken, NJ: John Wiley & Sons, 2006.

"Shaping the Global Agenda: The Shifting Power Equation," Proceedings of the 2007 Annual Meeting of the World Economic Forum, Davos, January 24–28, 2007.

Young, D., and S. O'Byrne. *EVA and Value-Based Management: A Practical Guide to Implementation.* New York: McGraw-Hill, 2000.

About the Author

Leo M. Tilman is President of L. M. Tilman & Co., a strategic advisory firm that serves governments, financial institutions, corporations, and institutional investors worldwide. L. M. Tilman & Co. provides a wide array of advisory services to executives, boards of directors, and leadership teams, specializing on the convergence of business strategy, corporate finance, investments, balance sheet management, and risk management under the umbrella of strategic decision-making. Prior to founding the firm, Mr. Tilman held senior positions with BlackRock as well as Bear Stearns, where he was Chief Institutional Strategist and Senior Managing Director.

Mr. Tilman teaches Finance at Columbia University, which is also his graduate and undergraduate alma mater. He is co-author of the book *The Risk Paradigm* (forthcoming from Oxford University Press in 2009), co-author of *Risk Management* (Wiley, 2000) that was translated into Chinese and Japanese, and editor of the book *Asset/Liability Management of Financial Institutions* (Institutional Investor, 2003).

Mr. Tilman is Contributing Editor of *The Journal of Risk Finance* and a frequent speaker at leading business schools and conferences worldwide. He serves on the advisory board of the Center on Capitalism and Society at Columbia University and on the board of directors of Atlantic Partnership. Mr. Tilman was honored by the World Economic Forum as a Young Global Leader, joining a select group of executives, public figures and intellectuals recognized for "their professional accomplishments, commitment to society, and potential to contribute to shaping the future of the world."

Index

3M, 113

Abitibi Consolidated, 113
Abu Dhabi Investment Authority, 62
Accounting earnings:
  case study, 142–144
  risk-adjusted economic performance and, 96
  strategic decision making and, 80
Active beta investing, 71
ADC Telecommunications, 113
ADIA, 106
Adjusted for loan loss provision, 146
AIG Risk Finance, 107
  business model transformations and, 106
Allianz:
  business model recalibrations and, 102, 103
  economic value creation and, 30
Allstate, 105, 106
American International Companies, 107
Analytics, 13
Apex Silver Mines, 113
Arbitrage Pricing Theory, 137
Asian financial crisis, 6
Asset strategies:
  economic performance and, 153
  strategic decisions and, 94, 95
Asset/liability committees (ALCOs), 152
  systematic risks and, 83
Asset-allocation strategies, 1, 99–101
Asset-backed commercial paper (ABCP), 117
Asset-backed securities, 141
Atomization of risks, 53
Attribution. *See* Economic performance attribution

Balance sheet arbitrage:
  business model recalibrations and, 102
  economic value creation and, 27–28, 30
  financial crises and, 21–22
  improving economic performance and, 82
  preservation of, 111
  risk-based economic performance equation and, 16
  as a risk-based model, 68–69
  static business models and, 18
Bank For International Settlements, 52
Bank of America:
  business model recalibrations and, 102, 103
  economic value creation and, 30
  write downs by, 62
The Bank of New York:
  business model recalibrations and, 102, 104
  economic value creation and, 30
Banks. *See also specific type*
B FIRST, 107
Bhide, Amar, x

The Blackstone Group:
  business model recalibrations and, 102, 103, 105
  economic value creation and, 30
Blue ocean strategies, xv, 136
Borrow, inability to, 24, 122–124
Bretton Woods, 13, 54
Brevan Howard Asset Management, 105
Bristol-Myers, 113
Brokers:
  compensation reduction for financial services and, 56
  static business models and, 20
Business model transformations, 99–101, 104–109
  responsive recalibrations and, 101–104
Buy-and-hold behavior, 42

Capital, costs of, 19, 21–22
Capitalism, dynamism and, x–xi
Capital structure:
  business model recalibrations and, 102, 104
  economic value creation and, 29–30
  optimization, 75
    improving economic performance and, 86
    risk-based economic performance equation and, 18
  strategic decisions and, 94, 95
Carry trades, 8–9, 115–118
  modern financial crises and, 120
Certificates of deposit, 145
Chandler, Alfred, x
China Investment Corporation, 62, 105, 106
Ciena, 113
Citigroup:
  business model recalibrations and, 105
  write downs by, 62
Collateralized debt obligations (CDOs), 61
College endowments, 106. *See also* Yale Endowment
Columbia University, Center on Capitalism and Society, xiii
Commercial banks:
  balance sheet arbitrage and, 69
  business model transformations and, 89–92, 106
  liabilities of, 76–77
  pressures on static business models and, 55–57, 64
  static business models and, 20, 41–42
Commercial mortgage-backed securities, 141
Complexity, 97
Consumer loans, 141, 145
Contagion, financial crises and, 23, 24, 122–124
Convergence, 13
  secular forces and, 52
Corporate bonds, 141, 145
Corporate finance, strategic decision making and, 80
Credit Agricole, write downs by, 62

169